82-

words *of* COURAGE *&* CONFIDENCE

sue patton thoele

BARNES & NOBLE BOOKS

NEW YORK

Published by MJF Books
Fine Communications
322 Eighth Avenue
New York, NY 10001

Words of Courage and Confidence
LC Control Number 2003116453
ISBN 1-56731-628-X

Manufactured in the United States of America on acid-free paper ∞

MJF Books and the MJF colophon are trademarks of Fine Creative Media, Inc.

VB   10 9 8 7 6 5   4   3   2   1

Contents

Everyday Courage and Confidence

I am deeply touched that the ideas and affirmations in *The Woman's Book of Courage* and *The Woman's Book of Confidence*—from which *Words of Courage and Confidence* have been complied—have passed the test of time and are still seen as words we can return to time and again for comfort, encouragement, and inspiration. It's been more than a decade since the original books were published, and each was a joy to write. However, I can't claim the credit for being much more than an organizer, typist, and story-gatherer because the ideas flowed through me as if from an unseen, insistent, and inexhaustible spring. I wrote or recorded ideas everywhere—in the car, standing in line at the DMV, in church, while showering, getting my hair cut . . . . Often, I found myself wide awake in the middle of the night compelled to get up and jot down an idea, exercise, story, or affirmation. There were nights when, bleary-eyed, I begged the Muse to leave me alone and let me sleep. Sometimes she obliged and saved her nudges until morning, but often she didn't.

I clearly remember one 4 A.M. when Gene, my sleep-drugged and worried husband, asked from my office door, "Is there *anything* I can do for you?" Short of clubbing me into unconsciousness, there wasn't. As a more seasoned writer, I now know being that on fire creatively—a willing but tired servant of the Muse—is a rare blessing, one to be treasured in the center of my soul.

With boundless gratitude to the Muse once again, I am thrilled to introduce *Words of Courage and Confidence* to you. Never before in my lifetime has our beleaguered world needed the power of Feminine Energy more than it does today. Only through the deep values of the Feminine, which are love, cooperation, acceptance, intuition, and inclusion, can peace and goodwill flower in the world. When we understand—as the Feminine Principal does—that we are all a part of the Whole and, therefore, need to be compassionately concerned for every being, including ourselves, will Mother Earth, and *all* people, receive the respect and compassionate consideration that they need and deserve.

How can we help? By being who we are! And by tapping into the courage and confidence inherent in all of us.

Courage is having the strength and willingness to overcome our resistance and do what we feel is right, even though it is difficult and/or we are afraid. It takes tremendous courage to face our fears, though it is essential that we do. For it is only when we free ourselves from the leg irons of fear, accepting and honoring the wisdom, strength, and beauty we naturally possess, that we can truly find the happiness we seek.

Confidence is another necessary element that will sustain this happiness. As it's been for many of us, gaining and sustaining self-confidence has been a continuing struggle for me. Only through learning to consistently treat myself lovingly have I been able to maintain a sense of enduring self-worth. Feelings of worthiness inevitably enhance confidence. Even though they are hard to do, the guided meditations and affirmations found in this book are very effective instruments for pulling us out of the black pit of low self-esteem.

These exercises and stories can help us act from the feminine values inherent within our womanhood and, thereby, create more compassion, respect, and understanding in the world as a whole. As we enhance our courage and become increasingly confident in ourselves, our beliefs, our ideas, and our contributions, we will naturally bring light into darkness, joy into sorrow, acceptance into judgment, and love into hate. Mustering the courage to bring our values to the fore and finding the confidence to stand resolutely behind them in the microcosm of our personal lives, will influence the macrocosm of planetary life as well.

If that sounds intimidating or impossible to you, as it once did to me, I understand. However, I've come to believe in the law of attraction that teaches "like attracts like." Countless experiences in my own life and in the lives of clients and friends have shown me that expressing positive energy attracts more positive energy to us. Love attracts love and respect engenders respect. Of course, the converse is also true; a sad fact that is exemplified in today's world where fear and intolerance are breeding more of the same.

The idea that we can make a difference is both encouraging and empowering. It gives us the oomph to keep on keeping on when the going gets tough and the future looks bleak. I fervently believe that changing negative beliefs and attitudes to ones that increase self-esteem and confidence, transforming debilitating fears, and acting with courageous integrity creates a hopeful and affirming atmosphere around us and helps diminish fear and unfairness elsewhere. Each small triumph we experience in our private life also widens the avenues toward freedom, security, and respect for the public as well. Every time we have the courage to speak up for ourselves, even if afraid to do so, a tiny energy-torch is lighted that illuminates the path toward peace and harmony for others. Each time we have the confidence to express and act on our ideas and beliefs, the energy supporting free expression is augmented. Our small daily choices make a big difference.

It is my hope that this book gives you more ways to easily make small daily choices with courage and confidence which can help you grow in ways you may have never imagined before. *Words of Courage and Confidence* can be used in many ways—as a meditation guide, a daily reminder, or to answer a specific question. You may want to open it at random, asking your higher self to guide you to the page that is right for you at this particular moment. Or you can use each of the sections as a weekly or monthly study guide.

Many of the affirmations and imagery in this book formed the basis of an ongoing women's group in which I took part for two years. We found it much easier to have the courage and confidence to change, because we supported and were supported by others who had similar goals and desires. Sharing our frustrations and celebrating our progress fostered and facilitated our growth. Maybe you will want to form a group of your own, using the concepts in *Words of Courage and Confidence* as springboards for discussion. It was a powerful experience for all of us. The group was a safe place where we learned to truly trust ourselves and each other.

Even if we have safe places to go, there are still times we become discouraged and doubtful that we can make a difference in the face of dysfunction, disinterest, or distress. At these times I recall my twelve-year-old-self's wonder at the change a single lighted match made in the complete darkness of Carlsbad Caverns. This memory prompts me to pray that the energy created by both my struggles and my successes will be used to help light the way for all those who grapple with similar issues and fears. Asking that my own turmoil's and triumphs be used for the greater good seems to lighten the load and give meaning and purpose to difficult times and circumstances.

The truth is, we probably all shine more brightly and effectively than we can ever imagine.

It is my hope and prayer that reading *Words of Courage and Confidence* will fan the flame in your heart that allows you to accept how wise and wonderful you are, helps you believe in your inherent courage, and brings the spark of confidence to each encounter of every day.

—Sue Thoele

Accepting What Is

I find that it is not the circumstances in which we are placed, but the spirit in which we meet them that constitutes our comfort.

—Elizabeth King

WHEN WE CAN ADOPT THE FOLLOWING SIMPLE BUT PRO-found prayer as our life's creed, we epitomize acceptance in its healthiest form: *God, grant me the serenity to accept the things I cannot change, the courage to change the things I can, and the wisdom to know the difference.*

Acceptance is a difficult lesson to learn. There are always conditions in our lives over which we have no control, and we can get stuck believing that circumstances should be a certain way in order to be acceptable, or that people must act in a prescribed fashion before we can find them acceptable. Caught in the intolerance of our *shoulds* and *have to's*, acceptance is canceled out. When we clutch resistance tightly to our chests and vow we'll never accept thus and so, we cement ourselves into the situation, attitude, or pain.

The acceptance I am talking about is not giving up or lapsing into hopeless resignation; it is having the wisdom to know when to say, "Ah, this is how it is. How can I have peace of mind in the face of this?"

Kicking the Approval Habit

ONE OF THE MOST INSIDIOUS ADDICTIONS WE WOMEN STRUGGLE with is our craving for approval from others. When our need for validation gets in the way of our being who we truly are, we're in trouble. Fueled by a belief that we need *their* approval in order to be okay, we scurry around looking for "self"-esteem fixes from suppliers that are outside of ourselves. It doesn't work.

Of course we all need people to appreciate us, but our primary source of approval needs to come from ourselves. The very best way to kick the approval habit is to support and approve of ourselves. This doesn't mean that we overlook our shortcomings or pat ourselves on the back for being nasty, but, in my many years of being a psychotherapist, I have seen very few people who err on the side of being too *easy* on themselves.

Authentic self-approval naturally leads to increased approval of others. Malia attracts friends like flowers attract bees. She is a heart-lifter; around her everyone feels better about themselves. She always seems to have a sincere word of praise for those around her.

But others are not the only recipients of her approval. She is also very self-confident and comfortable about bestowing accolades on herself. It's not unusual for her, in an unaffected and honest way, to say something like, "I am so proud of the way I handled that!" Asked if she had always been so kind to herself, she giggled, "Oh no, I used to be my own worst enemy, but I learned to be my own best friend instead!"

When we learn to accept who we are right now and celebrate who we are becoming, we can kick the approval habit and rely on ourselves for our best approval fixes.

I wholeheartedly approve of myself right now.

What others think of me is their choice;
what I think of me is my choice.

I easily approve of others.

Viewing Discipline As Desirable

ACCEPTING THE FACT THAT WE ARE RESPONSIBLE FOR OUR OWN LIVES is incredibly empowering. We may have been erroneously taught that we were in charge of making other people's lives happier, but few women have been encouraged to see that, in reality, we are responsible for making our own lives work. Accepting that "the buck stops here" so far as responsibility for our attitudes and accomplishments is concerned requires self-confidence—the awareness that we are capable and can do it, whatever *it* is at the moment.

If we are to maintain confidence in ourselves, we must be able to trust that we'll do what we say we're going to do. This requires a healthy amount of self-discipline—not the harsh and strict expectations a critical parent might have, but reasonable and *do-able* self-discipline—such as setting realistic goals and then following through with what we have agreed to do.

Although the word *discipline* sometimes evokes a negative response, it actually comes from the word **disciple**, meaning a learner who is in loving response to a respected teacher. Viewing ourselves as both a teacher and a learner simultaneously, not as an errant child in need of punishment, helps us do whatever needs doing.

During a quiet time when you will not be disturbed, allow yourself to focus on your breathing. Effortlessly deepen your breathing, relaxing more completely with each inhalation and exhalation. In this relaxed state, gently allow a sense or picture of a loving and respected teacher to come into your awareness. If the person or symbol that appears is not totally comfortable for you, ask it to leave and invite the perfect teacher to appear.

Take a few minutes to simply **be** with your teacher, basking in love and acceptance. Then discuss with your teacher an attitude or circumstance about which you are having difficulty being disciplined. Ask for assistance. Together, you will know how to create an environment where the needed discipline can blossom.

I enjoy being gently self-disciplined.

I accept responsibility for my life.

Sitting with "I Don't Know"

ENDURING THE UNKNOWN IS DRAINING FOR MOST OF US. WHETHER it is waiting for the results of a test, wondering about the outcome of a job interview, or questioning whether a particular relationship is healthy for us, we have a tendency to want the answer *now*. Especially difficult is having the patience and wisdom to allow our inner sorting process to happen naturally—sitting with our "I don't know"—rather than forcing ourselves into decisions and commitments before we really *know* what is best.

Just as babies take months to develop and seeds take days or weeks to sprout, most of our answers unfold from an internal questioning period in which the only honest and authentic reality is "I don't know." Our task is to accept this process as creative and productive, honor and embrace our questions, and trust that, if we allow it, the best choice will eventually evolve.

After moving to a new state, my husband and I were having difficulty finding a home we both liked. I found my dream spot, four acres with a gorgeous view, but Gene realized that four acres would require more work than either of us wanted to do. He then found what appeared to be a fair compromise, but I couldn't get excited about the new site. Having been a dedicated husband-pleaser for many years, it took a lot of courage for me to sit with my "I don't know" about the property. I wasn't sure if my resistance was intuition about what was right for us or rebellion over not getting the acreage I loved.

It would have been easy for me to capitulate and do what I felt Gene wanted, but I sat with the issue, sifting and sorting the pros and cons until I *knew*: the site was not for me. Luckily, a few patient weeks later, we found a lot that we *both* loved.

Although sitting with our "I don't knows" may feel like an endless free-fall, it allows our astute interior computer to gather the information necessary to make valid decisions.

I trust myself to make good decisions.

I honor my questions and patiently pursue my own answers.

Letting Go through Ritual

MANY UNACCEPTABLE THINGS HAPPEN TO US IN A LIFETIME. Paradoxically, in order to live life to the fullest, we must learn to accept all of life's incidents—the wonderful and the terrible. Accepting the unacceptable is so foreign and repulsive to our conscious mind that we often need to bypass it, through ritual, in order to impress our subconscious mind with our intention toward acceptance.

As a result of a routine mammogram, Frances found herself diagnosed, hospitalized, and without a breast before she was able to process her feelings let alone accept the unacceptable fact of having cancer. During her convalescence, Frances ran the emotional gamut from thankfulness for her life to despair over her appearance and the possible recurrence of the disease.

Dedicated to healing physically and emotionally, Frances decided to plan a letting-go ritual. She wanted to commemorate not only the loss of her breast, but all of the things she regretted losing or never having during her fifty years. After gathering pictures of herself that were representative of her regrets, she burned them in the backyard. Frances visualized the fire transforming those images of hurt, pain, and loss into more positive energy. To conclude, Frances buried the ashes and ceremoniously celebrated communion with herself as she watched the twilight deepen.

Scan your mind and feelings for anything you have not yet been able to accept. Ask yourself if you are honestly willing to let go of the pain and move on. If your answer is no, honor that— the time may not be right. But if you feel ready to release the pain, create a ritual for yourself that will notify your subconscious of the decision. When you sincerely wish to heal through ritual, the perfect way to do so will occur to you.

Accepting what is, even though it's not what we wish it to be, is letting go of all hope of a better yesterday. And that allows us to fully embrace today as it is.

*I give myself the gift of letting go of
the unchangeable past.*

I use ritual to heal the deepest parts of myself.

I am wise.

Accepting Who We Are

To accept who we are and who we are not is a fundamental invitation being issued continually from our higher selves. What a challenge! It is such a temptation to "if only" our acceptance to death: If only I were more successful . . . If only I were married (or single) . . . If only I were smarter, prettier, wiser . . . then I would be able to accept myself.

Because during our lifetime we are involved in a continual reincarnation of selves—being reborn regularly into new identities, new beliefs, new talents—it is imperative that we learn to accept ourselves *now*, as is. We may never get another chance to accept the self who looks back from the mirror today. By tomorrow she may be an entirely new person. If we accept her today, that new woman will be happier and more capable than the one who lives in our skin now.

My mother was a wise and talented woman who had a unique gift for listening intently and caring deeply for people. Yet she struggled her entire life to accept herself. I knew how many lives, including mine, she had touched in a loving way, and watching her wrestle with the demon of low self-esteem broke my heart. Because of her inability to accept herself as the truly wonderful person she was, Mother wondered, especially in the last months, if her life had been meaningful. Reassurances assuaged her doubts for a while, but they always returned.

The extent of her effect on people was underscored by the length of her funeral caravan winding its way to the cemetery. On the ride, I said silently to her, "Do you see those cars, Mom? Now can you accept and believe how wonderful you are?" The message I got back was filled with chuckles and exuberance and said, "Yes, Honey, you were right . . . *now* I can see it!"

Let us not wait until tomorrow—or eternity—to accept who we are. Let's do it right now.

I deserve acceptance from myself and others.

I am acceptable just as I am.

I accept myself.

Making Sacrifices

IN BOOKS AIMED AT HELPING WOMEN LEARN TO EMPOWER themselves, we are often warned about habitual self-sacrifice, but there are times when sacrificing individual desires is a valid way to honor who we truly are. In family crises, such as illness or loss of income, sacrificing our personal needs for the good of the whole is often the most appropriate and satisfying thing we can do.

Josie, an artist, is a good example of a woman who knows how to distinguish between appropriate and inappropriate service. For many years, her husband suffered from chronic kidney failure. Josie put her art, as well as her needs, on the back burner in order to care for her husband. Since she freely chose to make her husband and his health the priority, she experienced no resentment. In fact, because she reveled so much in his talent, sense of humor, and searching intellect, she felt she gained as much as she gave. Every day of her life Josie sacrificed and felt good about herself while doing so.

Six years ago Josie's husband died, and since then she has made a very conscious choice *not* to sacrifice for others but to put her own talents, wants, and needs on the front burner of her life. And that is the perfect choice for her now.

Our feelings are the most legitimate indicators of whether the sacrifices we're making are appropriate or inappropriate. If, for the most part, we feel good about our actions and decisions, it probably means that our sacrifice springs from *wanting* to serve. If, however, we consistently experience such feelings as anxiety, resentment, or anger, our sacrifice may come from believing we have no other option.

If you are feeling used and abused while sacrificing, it is important to find someone with whom you can talk freely. The right listener can help you explore your feelings, attitudes, and options. As women who have historically been designated the care-givers, our big challenge is knowing when our inclination toward sacrifice and service is appropriate and when it is not.

I make wise choices.

When necessary and appropriate, I sacrifice
from a full and loving heart.

Riding in the Change Parade

OUR LIVES ARE A CONSTANT PARADE OF CHANGES! SOME WILL BE inspiring and exciting, making us want to grab our baton, jump in front of the band, and shout for joy. Others will more closely resemble a funeral cortege. In light of its inevitability, befriending change is a comforting philosophy for us to work toward. By looking for the personal growth inherent in any new phase of life, we can make the Change Parade work for us rather than against us.

Doggedly resisting change sets us up to be forever fighting the inescapable, which can eventually lead to feelings of hopelessness and depression. When we master the art of accepting change and commit to making the best of it, we are choosing to evolve—to be vital, useful, and happier people.

I recently read an inspiring story about a courageous teenager from whom we can learn a lot about assimilating change. Sixteen-year-old cancer patient Beth was given two choices: radiate the tumor and hope the cancer would die, or amputate her foot and keep the disease from spreading. Beth made the decision to "take it off." While her optimistic outlook faltered when she saw the stump for the first time, one day the crying stopped and, as Homecoming Princess, she hobbled out onto the field in her cheerleading outfit to admiring applause from the crowd.

In the Change Parade of her young life, Beth not only *walked* on her new artificial foot but, a year and a half after surgery, she—and the eleven other members of her squad—twirled, scissor-kicked, jumped, and danced her way to a Class A State Cheerleading Championship.

When Beth was asked what she had learned, she answered, "You can take any situation and make it better by bringing yourself up." As Beth's courageous acceptance of her situation shows, the Grand Marshall in the Change Parade of our lives is often greater courage and expanded compassion. You too can bring yourself up!

I have the courage to accept change.

I allow change to teach me valuable lessons.

Making It through the Rain

WE ALL KNOW, OR KNOW OF, INSPIRING PEOPLE WHO SEEM TO weather life's greatest storms in the most growth-producing ways. Leslie, a single mother, is such a person. At thirty-two she was stricken with a rare and usually fatal form of cancer. When first diagnosed, she was panic stricken and enraged, bereft at the thought of not seeing her daughter grow up. Understandably, she sank into a depression.

As Leslie puts it, one day she *awoke* from her depression with the awareness that her life force, or life flame as she calls it, was not yet extinguished. In that illuminating moment, she realized that it was up to her to protect her life flame from this life-threatening deluge. She began to meditate regularly, and at length, on the light in each cell of her body—even the cancer cells—centering on transforming the cancer cells rather than destroying them.

Leslie supported her life force by learning to love and appreciate herself exactly as she was, and then concentrated on transforming the destructive cells with the light of love. Hope and faith became Leslie's slicker in this storm, and self-acceptance and understanding were the umbrellas protecting her flickering life flame.

When faced with almost certain death, Leslie realized how desperately she wanted to learn to lovingly accept herself and her family in ways she hadn't been able to before. With that goal in mind, Leslie did make it through the rain. Today she is healthy, but she says that so sincere was her acceptance of herself and her illness, that she would have been at peace even if death had been the outcome.

Into each life a little rain must fall. All of us will experience storms during our lifetime, and we all have the inner strength and wisdom to weather them with grace. We can make it through the rains more easily when we greet them protected by self-love, acceptance, and support.

I lovingly accept myself.

I weather the storms of life gracefully.

I learn to better understand myself during stormy times.

Changing What Can Be Changed

You may be disappointed if you fail, but you're doomed if you don't try.

—*Beverly Sills*

IMAGINE WHAT IT WOULD BE LIKE IF THE OWNER OF AN aquarium never changed the water in the tank. It wouldn't be long before the fish died attempting to glean oxygen from a stagnant and used-up source. Changing the water and keeping it circulating allows marine animals to thrive in their habitat. It's much the same with us. Without change we would stagnate.

Although many of us resist it fiercely, change forces us to grow and evolve, to become more flexible, resilient, and confident. Our task is to transcend any fear of the unknown and encourage ourselves to change what needs to be different in our lives in order for them to flow freely and creatively.

A wonderful Zen story tells of a teacher giving a student a silk scarf snarled in many knots. The student's assignment was to free the scarf of the knots, a chore he struggled with until receiving the insight that, in order to succeed, he must untie the knots in reverse order.

Change can be difficult, but when we trust ourselves to untie each little knot, in the right order, our entire scarf can eventually be freed to flutter gently in the breeze.

Knowing We Are in Charge
of Our Attitudes

IN THE FACE OF UNCOMFORTABLE CIRCUMSTANCES, SOMETIMES THE only thing we have the power to change is our mind. During times when we feel out of control, we can comfort ourselves by remembering, as the Reverend June Kelly says, "We are the *only* author of our thoughts—the only thinker in our lives." *We* are in charge of our attitudes. Since feelings are a direct result of attitudes and thoughts, the ability to change our minds is one of our most precious and useful attributes.

Society encourages us to be what it considers *realistic,* and there are even semiderisive descriptions for those people with positive attitudes: cockeyed optimist, Pollyanna, and ivory-tower idealist to name a few. But why is it cockeyed to be optimistic? Why isn't a tendency to expect the best possible outcome wise, rather than naive or stupid?

A dedicated realist might answer that we are only setting ourselves up for disappointment when we habitually expect the best; I would respond by saying that a negative or pessimistic attitude, masquerading as realism, ensures us discouragement as we apprehensively wait for the ax to fall.

Ariel graduated from college two years ago and, following a successful internship, went out to find a job. Many realists presented her with grim statistics on the limited market for her skills. At first she felt almost paralyzed with discouragement.

A good talk with her mother helped Ariel realize she needed to change her attitude, focusing instead on how fortunate any company would be to have her as an employee. When pessimism crept in during particularly frustrating periods in her job search, Ariel reassured herself by choosing to remember what she had to give, rather than concentrating on what she feared she had to lose. Although it took a while, Ariel is now employed full-time in her field.

Knowing we are in charge of our attitudes is one of the most life-enhancing realizations we can come to.

I am an optimist and proud of it.

I choose to expect the best.

Reframing Reality

THERE ARE THOSE OF US WHO SEE REALITY ONLY BY THE HARSH GLARE of television news coverage or in the unknowable shadows of "what if . . . ." Because the news seems to accentuate the negative, and the unknown is often so frightening, is it any wonder that one of our society's primary diseases is depression?

But the good news is that we can reframe reality. We can choose what we look at, listen to, and respond to. Yes, negative things happen. Yes, there is much pain and suffering—in the world and in our own lives—and we need to have compassion for it. But we don't have to become irretrievably entangled in it to the detriment of our own happiness. The French novelist Colette summed up this choice when she said, "What a wonderful life I've had. I only wish I'd realized it sooner."

We can realize how wonderful our lives are by changing what we focus on—how we frame our reality. An elderly friend of mine said that calling herself a housewife didn't seem to command the respect she felt it deserved so she changed her title. When asked what she did, she responded that she was a social arbitrator. Not only did others seem more impressed by her career choice, but *she* believed it to be a much fairer description of her role and therefore felt more valued.

Quietly think of a situation in your life that you consider difficult or depressing. Allow your creative mind to take a snapshot of it. Now bring into your awareness the frame that you have this situation in. Is it dark and heavy? Huge and cumbersome? Covered with ugly decorations? Ask yourself how you would like to frame this situation. Allow a new frame to appear, one more manageable and maybe even beautiful. What change in attitude will you need in order to reframe your picture? When this situation next arises, take a moment to see it in the context of your new frame.

As we learn to reframe our reality, our lives can become filled with the fantastic, heaped with heroes, and loaded with love.

I choose to see how wonderful my life is.

I have the power to reframe my reality.

I appreciate my life and all its variations.

Facing the Fork in the Road

WHILE STANDING AT A FORK IN THE ROAD, WONDERING WHAT CHOICE to make, it is important to take into account what is really right for us. So many of us women almost automatically say, "Whatever *you* want," as we stand on the threshold of a decision. Such self-denying, and often unconscious, behavior can cover the spectrum from a simple acquiescence, such as not choosing a restaurant, to a major sacrifice, such as giving up a career because someone else disapproves or may be inconvenienced.

Perhaps at a crossroad in our lives we disowned an important dream, ignored the yearning of our hearts, or simply did not do for ourselves what we would automatically have done for a friend. Regrets are born from the resultant feelings of self-betrayal.

Sit quietly for a few minutes and focus entirely on your breathing. If your mind wanders, as it probably will, very gently return your attention to your breath, gradually allowing it to deepen. With each inhalation, sense your body's gratitude for this clean air. As you exhale, feel yourself relaxing. Invite into your mind's theater a circumstance in your life that feels like a fork in the road. Carefully observe how you feel and act when faced with the decision of which path to follow. Explore your fears, expectations, and hopes concerning each road. Quietly ask yourself what route is best for you. If your answer is a quagmire of contradictions, concentrate on your breath once again until you feel relaxed.

After recentering yourself, write the question: What is the right decision for me in this instance? Jot down your first thought. Follow that with the simple question, Why? and list your reasons, to help affirm your choice. We know what is best for us and when we allow ourselves to really listen to our inner wisdom, we can turn a fork in the road into a genesis of self-respect and self-esteem.

*I have the strength to handle the consequences
and the rewards of my choices.*

I know what is best for me and act accordingly.

Defibrillating Our Funny Bone

IF WE DISCOVER THAT RESPONSIBILITY AND SERIOUSNESS HAVE shuttled our sense of humor off into cold storage, where it has atrophied from lack of use, we can rescue and revive it. We have the power to decide to change our outlook—lighten it up, let it bubble rather than grumble.

Sometimes our funny bone, as well as our zest for life, gets buried under fear of ridicule or disillusionment. Hilary, whose mother often cautioned her against getting too excited about anything for fear she would be disappointed, is a good example of entombed enthusiasm. Having been disappointed often in her own life, Hilary's mother felt she was doing her daughter a favor by saving her from the same grief she had experienced. As she grew up, Hilary took her mother's advice and tightly controlled her emotions and anticipations until her life felt flat and leveled. Safe, but dull and joyless.

Feeling that life must hold more passion than this, Hilary decided she wanted to defibrillate her funny bone and invite humor and excitement back into her life. As an affirmation, she purchased a personalized license plate that says GTXCITD. Each time Hilary sees her car she's reminded that it's all right—and even much healthier—to *get excited*.

Even if we have temporarily forgotten that life can be pretty darned funny a lot of the time, we can *choose* to remember to take everything less seriously, patch our levity leaks, and let laughter lighten our load. Humor and enthusiasm are *natural*! If we're not experiencing them it's because we have buried our inherent impulse to *play*.

It might help to find a symbol of playfulness—a picture, a balloon, a clown pin, a puppy or unicorn sticker, whatever—and carry it with you. Glancing at the symbol and consciously reminding yourself that it is okay to play can help resuscitate your levity.

It is up to us to defibrillate our funny bone. Only we have the means to get out our defibrillation paddles, turn on the juice, and then let 'er rip. We *can* GTXCITD.

I love life.

I have a great sense of humor.

I love to laugh and get excited.

Carving Our Own Niche

WOMEN HAVE COME A LONG WAY SINCE A.D. 1500, WHEN SPANISH women were allowed to leave the house only three times: for their baptism as infants, to move into their husband's home, and to be buried.

Attitudes have changed a great deal since those repressive times, and men and women alike are now involved in a gentle (and, sometimes, not so gentle) revolution toward realness. We are working on finding our individual freedom by searching out what is right for each of us, free of stereotypes.

If we're to feel we are living our own life, not someone else's, it is imperative that we honor our unique calling. Dr. Elisabeth Kübler-Ross, the expert on death and dying, wisely noted, "The saddest people I see die are people who thought they could buy love by doing what mom and dad told them to do. They never listened to their own dreams. And they look back and say, 'I made a good living, but I never lived.'"

As she was growing up, Maureen loved playing with tools that were designated "boys' toys" by her parents. She liked building things; hammering and nailing boards together was a thrill. Her parents were horrified and, because she wanted and needed their approval, she abandoned her desire to build things. When she grew up, although it was not where her heart lay, Maureen became a secretary, a job looked upon as suitable by her parents. She was miserable.

Fortunately, Maureen awoke to the fact that she deserved to carve her own niche and, with the help of a therapist who assisted her in finding ways to communicate her true desires firmly but lovingly to her parents, became a carpenter.

In order to be our most creative selves, we need to accept the responsibility of carving out our own niche—searching for and seizing the activities and situations that are best suited to our unique abilities and aspirations.

I have a right to live my life.

I allow other people to be their own unique selves.

I give myself permission to follow my heart.

Colorizing Black and White

THERE ARE MANY OLD-MOVIE FANS, MYSELF INCLUDED, WHO LAMENT the colorization of black-and-white films. It dilutes their charm. However, there is nothing charming about running old black-and-white movies in our minds, in the form of absolutes and inflexibilities, or archaic opinions about ourselves. We need to colorize those, to bring in shades, shadows, and perhaps some pastels, for there are exceptionally few pure whites and true blacks in real life.

Seeing issues only in black and white tends to rigidify our attitudes and beliefs. In order to develop our potential, we need to remain flexible and willing to change. Colorizing interior movies helps us gain perspective on our problems and discern whether our underlying assumptions are in need of updating. Since it's often true that we don't see things as they are, but as we are, it's important for our emotional, mental, and spiritual unfolding that we be able to see with technicolor eyes.

Shirley was tearfully telling me how conflicted she was about the decision she and her husband had made about moving to a smaller house. She oscillated between being okay and being sad and enraged. I asked her what made her unhappy, and she was surprised to realize that she was running an old movie in her mind of a sacrificing victim who never got what she wanted.

With further probing, Shirley realized that she had healed enough to never return to her old pattern of totally giving herself away, but the old black-and-white movie was still cranking away. She colorized it by remembering, and giving herself credit for, the new self-supporting behaviors she is now consistently doing.

Allowing ourselves to move from seeing only black and white into being able to distinguish shades of gray means it's only a matter of time, desire, and commitment before we can add bright colors to previously stark perspectives.

I see my life in bright and beautiful technicolor.
I let go of useless and restrictive beliefs and attitudes.

Observing and Elevating Thoughts

BECAUSE WE ARE SENTENCED TO THE CONSEQUENCES OF OUR accumulated thoughts, it is important that we learn to observe and elevate them. Since thoughts are energy, they draw to them the same stuff they are made of. Therefore, if our thoughts are tin, what we draw to us will feel tinny and uncomfortable—sort of like chewing on aluminum foil.

All of us have nasty thoughts—critical, ugly, hateful, vengeful, intolerant, prejudiced—for we are human. And by observing and elevating our thoughts I'm not suggesting that we repress or sugarcoat our negative ones. If we do that, we empower them by pushing them into the deep recesses of our subconscious mind where they only grow stronger. I am suggesting that we not get attached to shadowy thoughts, but, rather, notice them and let them go. Being horrified and shamed by our negative thoughts can indelibly tattoo them on our psyches, whereas nonjudgmentally observing them for a moment allows thoughts to flow through and out of our minds.

For instance, I recently had the flu, and each time I caught myself dwelling on how lousy I felt, I tried to remember to replace that thought in a couple of different ways. First, I gave thanks for the incredible healing machine that my body is, and affirmed that this, too, shall pass. Second, I visualized my body using this illness as an opportunity to cleanse and release all the toxins that had accumulated over the preceding year. Although elevating my thoughts to a plain higher than my physical discomfort did not cure the illness, it did improve my attitude and keep my optimism intact.

As an exercise in helping you observe and elevate your thoughts, imagine that everyone can read your mind. When a negative thought comes into your mind that you would rather keep to yourself, acknowledge it nonjudgmentally and then replace it with an uplifting one. Moving our thoughts to higher ground supports change in our lives.

*I encourage negative thoughts to move
rapidly through me.*

My thoughts align with the purpose of my higher self.

Kicking the Worry Habit

WORRY IS A HABIT THAT KNOCKS THE SUPPORTS RIGHT OUT FROM under us. So one of the most freeing changes we can make in our lives is to kick the worry habit. Since most habits are learned, it's important for us to ask where we learned to worry.

Rosa was a chronic worrier who came to see me in the hope that she could find relief from depression and insomnia. She said, "I was raised on worry and secondhand smoke, and I inhaled and absorbed the worry every bit as much as I did the smoke."

We explored the often unspoken but nevertheless powerful beliefs Rosa's parents had bequeathed. The majority of them were based on the assumptions that life was difficult, money was hard to come by, and God was a stern and punishing father. Rosa learned to believe that it never rained but it poured, there was never enough to go around, and that guilt was the only thing that could convince a vengeful God not to condemn her. Is it any wonder Rosa became a worrier?

The only lasting antidote for chronic worry is faith, faith in the good, faith that the Universal Mystery is for us rather than against us. If we have learned to believe in the unfortunate and hateful, we have the ability to change that and come to believe in goodness and love. I know it's possible because Rosa did it, and so did I. As Rosa was starting to change her belief system, I gave her a little card that read, *Sometimes we have many reasons to be unhappy and not many reasons to be happy. Our task is to be unreasonably happy.*

If you are plagued by the worry habit, simply becoming aware of worry when it overtakes you and deciding to affirm that life is good will set your feet firmly on the road to kicking the worry habit.

What we believe is our choice and we can support ourselves by choosing to be faith-filled and happy—even unreasonably so.

I am safe.

God, the ultimate Mystery, loves and supports me.

I believe that life is good.

Taming the Coyote in the Henhouse

OUR DAYS CAN BE FILLED WITH SUCH FRENETIC ACTIVITY THAT PEACE of mind is lost and we feel as though we have stepped on a treadmill that is going way too fast. For our own well-being, we need to find ways to calm ourselves and slow down.

After hosting a wonderfully exuberant weekend party, I was so keyed up that I couldn't work or sleep. I felt like a coyote was in the henhouse of my mind and all the chickens were squawking and flapping madly in a cloud of feathers.

Needing to settle my feathers, I took a long, brisk walk to dissipate excess physical energy and then called a loving friend to share how scattered I felt. Only after exercise and expressing my feelings was I able to center myself through meditation. I created a peaceful atmosphere—candles, silence, and a view of nature— and sat down to meditate.

What is peaceful and conducive to contemplation for you? How often do you allow yourself the luxury (or, it could be argued, the *necessity*) of uninterrupted tranquil time? If you don't often experience rejuvenating solitude in which serenity can blossom, now is the time to give yourself the boon of allowing that.

After establishing a setting that is soothing to you, rest in it. Give yourself permission to simply *be* in the place you have made. There are no rules. Just be you. After several minutes of quiet, visualize your mind's activity. You may want to use my coyote/henhouse analogy or anything else that seems appropriate to you. Consciously encourage your mind to rest. Gently, slowly, as though watching a storm abate, create a calmer atmosphere. If the whirlwind persists, tenderly assure your mind that it's okay to be quiet and allow it to respond positively to that suggestion.

Although it isn't easy to do in our scattered and scattering environment, we have the power to tame the coyote in the henhouse and create mental and emotional harmony out of pandemonium.

I am calm and peaceful.

Serenity is possible even in the midst of chaos.

Using Our Rage

HARNESSING THE FORCE OF OUR RAGE AS WE HARNESS AND DAM flowing water in order to create electricity is a powerful way for women to institute needed changes in society. I believe rage is different than anger in that it touches feelings more intense than anger and is more universal. It is a mighty force that can be used for our benefit when channeled constructively. Rage is the consequence of cumulative disrespect and devaluation. Anger fumes for *us*, whereas rage flares for the *whole*.

Rachel was involved in a fender bender and felt mildly irritated with the other driver, who was at fault, because of the inconvenience the accident would create for her. However, when he jokingly made a remark to the policeman about women drivers, she was instantly catapulted into rage. What in her had been triggered by that remark? Perhaps a profound resentment at the casual putdowns women endure or maybe an intense rebellion against the feminine being devalued by the masculine. Whatever the reason, a core issue of Rachel's was ignited and rage was the result. Luckily for the rest of us women, she did not keep silent about her feelings, and the outcome of her speaking up was an apology from the other driver.

Virginia Woolf's statement, "Scratch a woman and you'll find a rage" is indicative of our unwillingness to allow injustice to reign. Rage is the fuel of revolution. We women, with fires burning deeply in our hearts over the ills in our world, country, community, and in our own homes, have the ability to be a revolutionary force to be reckoned with as we fight for love, personal freedom, and an awareness of the connectedness of all persons and things.

Instead of dousing the flames of our rage, let us, with deep commitment, fan the embers and coolly, calmly, lovingly dam and direct our rage for the good of ourselves, others, and Mother Earth. May the conscious flow of our collective rage light the path for new supportive attitudes and irrigate our collective conscience with ideas of equality for *all*.

*I have the courage to speak up
when faced with injustice.*

*I have the wisdom and the right to use
my rage constructively.*

Keeping Relationships Current

RECENTLY ONE OF MY DEAREST FRIENDS GAVE ME A VERBAL BOUQUET of roses. We were saying goodbye after a lengthy, heart-filling long-distance conversation when I said, "Words can't describe how much I love you, you know!" and she answered, "No, but your behavior does, on a consistent basis."

I was struck by how incredibly true her statement was about all relationships. Does our behavior match our commitment to another? Do we keep valued relationships current through attention and caring or do we get caught up in the whirlpool of busyness and ignore people we love?

Relationships are as important to us women as the very air we breathe. Without relationships we feel bereft, cut off from vital sources of comfort and support. Yet, with our busy schedules, have we been able to make it a priority to keep our relationships current? Luckily, most of our heart-held relationships, those that add to our lives and multiply our blessings, are fairly drought-resistant and can thrive on bursts of concentrated love and attention. But if nurturing and sustaining our relationships feels like yet another energy-draining obligation, we need to change our perception and see friendship as a sacred, life-enhancing gift we give and receive.

Elizabeth Yates wrote a beautiful passage in her book *Up the Golden Stair*, "Keep your relationships current. Follow the impulse to do that small kindness for another whenever it comes to you. Then you will never be beset by the thought, Oh, if I had only done it when I thought of it—This is one of the discoveries I have made this year: that if the inner promptings of heart and mind are obeyed there will never be an echo of the words 'too late.'"

Open your heart for a moment and allow your intuition to clue you in to who needs a supportive word from you today. What kindness, compliment, or moment of your time can you give to someone with whom you want to keep your relationship current?

I nurture and sustain my relationships through following my urges to give.

I am a trustworthy friend to myself and others.

Acknowledging Strength and Setting Limits

Feminism called upon me to have the courage to grow up, to discover and exercise my womanly strength, to be unafraid of pain— and the pain is immeasurable—knowing that fully experienced, it makes joy fully possible.

—Sonia Johnson

OUR DAILY LIVES ARE PROOF OF OUR INHERENT STRENGTH. We women move through uncharted occupational territory, have and care for children, nurture others emotionally and physically, and explore our psychological and spiritual dimensions. Although we are usually strong for others, we often feel weak and victimized while attempting to set realistic limits that respect us as individuals. However, every human being has limits and, if we do not honor ours, we can become overextended, resentful, and even ill. So sometimes the most courageous thing we can do is be aware that we can't do it all for everyone.

Even when others disagree, it is important that we remember we have the right to be strong and to say no. When we know in our hearts that it is okay for us to honor ourselves by having limits, we can set them in a gentle way. Although it is one of the most difficult things women have to learn, often the courageous and loving thing for us to do is to acknowledge our strength and learn to set honest limits.

Imagining Ourselves Strong

WE ALL FACE SITUATIONS IN WHICH WE FEEL POWERLESS AND AFRAID.
I once had a client who was terrified of an upcoming child cus-
tody hearing. She felt intimidated by the legal system, her lawyer,
and especially her ex-husband. I asked her what it would take for
her to feel safe and strong in the court room.

"Nothing short of riding in on a brahman bull!" she answered jokingly. It was a great idea, straight out of her inner wisdom.

I had her work with the image. She had fun creating the scenario
of herself galloping into the court on a huge, snorting bull that
threatened to gore anyone who tried to frighten her. Her day in
court was a success because each time she felt the least bit scared
she visualized herself astride her bull. With the help of her amus-
ing but effective mental imagery she felt strong and capable. As a
result, she was treated as if she were powerful, someone not to be
dismissed or manipulated.

As the story illustrates, we are all as strong as we imagine ourselves to be. When we act as if we are strong, we move towards
becoming the powerful women we desire to be. Having the courage
to see ourselves as strong, capable, and wise, able to do what we
need and want helps make it so. But we need not do it alone. We
can move creatively through our fears by accepting support and
guidance from an unseen helper, whether that is a higher power or
a brahman bull.

I am strong and capable.
I can do whatever I set my mind to.
I am filled with strength and confidence.

Acting in Spite of Fear

TO ACT EVEN THOUGH WE ARE AFRAID is to be courageous. Amazingly, we do it almost every day. If we did not do what we feared, how many of us would move to a new state or decide to change jobs? More importantly, how many of us would be grappling with the intense need to be our own person if we were not, indeed, already courageous?

For years Fiona had felt at the mercy of her husband's temper. She was terrified by his outbursts; faced with his fury, she would appease him, suppressing her own feelings in the hopes he would calm down. Finally, cautiously she began to work on setting limits in her relationship. She talked to a therapist and went to Al-Anon meetings to help her have the courage to break the destructive pattern she was in with her husband. She knew she had succeeded when, on the eve of a trip to Hawaii, her husband blew up and said they were not going. Calmly, she continued to pack. With sadness but without anger, she told him she was sorry he felt as he did because she had been looking forward to a second honeymoon with him, but that she was going without him.

Getting to that point took tremendous courage for Fiona. She faced her fears and triumphed. Her story has a happy ending, too—her husband apologized for his outburst and they had a wonderful time in Hawaii.

Take a moment now to focus on your courageous acts. They can be very simple. If you are grieving, depressed, or otherwise in pain, it may take quite a bit of courage to do something as simple as getting out of bed or making dinner. Take a few moments to make a list of times when you have acted in spite of fear and then share your list with someone you trust. We are courageous every day, but it helps to remind us when we share our courage with others.

I have the courage to act even though
I feel afraid.

I have the strength to do the things
I need to do.

Knowing We Are Not the Target

WE OFTEN ALLOW OURSELVES to be deeply wounded by the actions of people around us. We feel guilty and irrationally think that it is our fault if people treat us badly. It takes courage not to do this.

Sarah's father and sister were invariably doing and saying things that wounded her deeply. She felt somehow responsible for their actions and became mired in guilt. One day, while visiting the zoo, she saw a gorilla bellowing and throwing excrement at onlookers. She realized that while she was among the crowd, she wasn't being personally targeted. Sarah decided to view the attacks of her father and sister in the same way. Now, when Sarah finds herself believing she is the target of her family's anger or manipulation, she pretends she is at the zoo observing another species and emotionally moves out of the line of fire.

It takes strength to know that we are not to blame for the actions of others, and that we do not need to be their target. Even if people insist on projecting their unfinished business onto us, we can train ourselves to remember that we are not responsible for what anyone else does or says. We can learn to take the bull's eye off our chest and put it in the closet.

I have the strength to know I am not the target.

I know I don't need to "fix"
anyone else's attitude or circumstances.

I dodge anger that is inappropriately aimed at me.

Chewing Bite-Size Pieces

MANY TIMES OUR AUTOMATIC REACTION WHEN FACED WITH AN uncomfortable or confusing situation is to thrash around trying to change it immediately. We attempt to swallow the whole predicament at once and spit it out, solved. Very rarely does this approach ease our pain or alter the situation. In fact, thoughtless, quick action is often more frustrating than productive.

When baffled or upset, we need to PAUSE, take a deep breath, and have the courage to recognize that we are intelligent and resourceful enough to solve the problem. We can either figure out a solution ourselves or find the people to help us. Slowly and thoughtfully, we can then begin to explore the problem and its possible solutions in bite-size pieces. Usually, as each small piece is solved, anxiety subsides and the entire puzzle fits together more easily than we might have feared.

Who, for instance, hasn't experienced qualms of inadequacy and frustration when first faced with a convoluted income tax form or an incomprehensible insurance form? Without a small-step approach to such chores, we can feel discouraged before we even start. But if we pause, take a deep breath and affirm our ability to solve our problem, then divide our task into small pieces, we can almost always conquer whatever is in front of us.

We can find what we need to solve our problems if we don't allow ourselves to become overwhelmed. Three little slogans we can use to remind ourselves of this are: Pause, don't panic; this isn't an emergency; I rarely choke on bite-size pieces.

I am resourceful.
I take one thing at a time in bite-size pieces.
I solve problems with ease and intelligence.

Putting Our White Horse out to Pasture

WOMEN TEND TO BE HABITUAL RESCUERS. WE LEAP ON OUR WHITE horses at the first sign of distress, believing that it is our job to save everyone. It isn't.

I was giving a talk at our local hospice meeting about how tiring it is to get stuck in the "rescue" mode. One woman volunteer exhaustedly said, "I agree, but what if your white horse is parked next to your husband's mule?" This woman had let herself be labeled The-One-Who-Fixes-It in her marriage, and her husband was stubbornly refusing to have it any other way. I asked her, "Do you believe you need to keep rescuing him?" Her answer was a hesitant, "Well, no, but. . . " Even though she was complaining, she really did believe it was her job. And of course, she couldn't get out of the position until she gave up her belief.

In reality, no one can rescue anyone else. Everyone must find his or her own way through life. However, breaking the white-horse habit is very difficult and takes commitment on our part. We need to keep reminding ourselves that, although society has fostered the myth of woman-as-rescuer, it is invalid. As we have the courage to continually halt our white horse in mid-gallop we will, in time, believe it is okay to do so.

I know I can rescue only myself.
I put my white horse out to pasture.
I trust others know how best to live their lives.

Crediting Our Life's Account

THE MYRIAD OF DEMANDS ON OUR TIME and energy can leave us feeling emotionally drained and physically exhausted. We become imbalanced when we give out more than we take in. Because women have been taught to be givers and receiving seems selfish to us, it takes enormous courage to see the value in allowing ourselves to give only that which is reasonable and healthy.

If your life were a bank account, how many daily deposits and withdrawals do you make to and from the account of your body, feelings, mind, and spirit? In fact, we all do have a "life account," from which we frequently make too many withdrawals or allow others to withdraw too freely.

In order to have a comfortable "balance" in our lives, we need to credit liberally and debit wisely. When we overdraw physically, emotionally, mentally, or spiritually, we "see red"; i.e., we experience frustration, anger, and exhaustion. But when we credit our life's account by setting realistic limits, we have more to give. Although taking care of ourselves is often difficult to do, it is an excellent investment in creating the quality of life we want and deserve. By taking the time to nurture ourselves, we ensure that we will not get "overdrawn."

I credit my "life account"
by setting realistic limits.

I have the courage to decide
what I will give and what I will not give.

My life is blessed
by balance and harmony.

KISSING Our Life

"YES" IS A LITTLE WORD, BUT IT CAN LEAD TO LOTS OF complications in our lives if we use it too liberally. Saying "No" is particularly hard for women because we feel guilty turning down requests or demands. We want to live up to our own and others' expectations, even if they are unreasonable.

How often do you find yourself overwhelmed by more commitments than you can comfortably handle, wondering, "Why did I say 'Yes' to this commitment? I knew I didn't really want to do it." One of the biggest reasons we say "Yes" is because we don't honor our limits—many of us aren't even aware of them until it's too late. But we all need to give ourselves permission to be aware of our limits, to listen to the inner warnings as they come, and then honor our wisdom by saying "No."

One way to begin to do this is to implement the old KISS philosophy of Keep It Simple, Sweetie. Say "No" to complexity and "Yes" to simplicity in your life. Complexity is exhausting and fragmenting while simplicity is energizing and centering.

Write a list of ways you can simplify your life. What obligations can you delegate to others, give up altogether, or modify in order to be comfortable with your commitments and feel you have not overstepped your limits? Gently close your eyes and visualize yourself living more simply. Having weeded out unnecessary responsibilities and commitments from your schedule, think of things you find nourishing, such as solitude, friendship, or romance, and visualize yourself enjoying them. We deserve to have a simply beautiful life.

I am aware of my limits and I honor them.
I give myself permission to keep my life simple.
I create the time to do things which nourish me.

Saying "No" without Feeling Guilty

WHAT IN THE WORLD IMPELS US TO SAY "YES" WHEN WE FEEL "NO"? We think we should. We're afraid of what they will think of us if we don't do what they want.

Vickie tearfully lamented to me, "I knew it wouldn't work when Jack (her husband) asked if he could come to work for me. Now he's there and I hate it! Why did I say "Yes?" Vickie had been taught to feel guilty if she refused a request. She is not alone—we women have been brainwashed to ignore what we feel is right for us if it doesn't comply with what others want. That's why it takes a lot of courage to stand up for ourselves and set limits; if we don't we can end up filled with regret and resentment, as Vickie did.

Even though we are afraid of disappointing others, when we really feel we have a right to say "No" and say it with full awareness of that right, people usually think it's just fine. For when we expect people to accept our No's and to honor our limits, they generally do. Our conviction that we have the right to choose to say "No" comes across and is accepted.

So we need to respectfully pay attention to ourselves, tuning in when the little voice inside wants to say "No." We are our own best experts. We can replace our draining shoulds with empowering words like can, want to, choose to, or will.

I have the right to say "No"
without feeling guilty.

I have the courage to say "No"
without feeling guilty.

I pay attention to what I know is right for me.

Retiring Aunt Jemima

LURKING IN THE SUBCONSCIOUS OF SOME WOMEN is the archaic belief that as a woman, wife, and mother, our proper role is willing servant to our families. Mindy came face to face with her hidden belief about the role she felt she played when she saw her family's Christmas photo. The idea had been for each family member to dress in outfits that indicated one of their main interests. The children were dressed in sports uniforms or theatrical costumes, and her husband wore his jogging togs. Mindy had chosen Aunt Jemima. She thought she dressed as a slave for a joke, but, after seeing the picture and thinking about her reasons for choosing as she did, she became aware that she really did feel like a slave. And she began to comprehend how resentful she felt as a result.

Realizing the role she had allowed herself to slip into was a turning point in her life. She decided to send Aunt Jemima into retirement. She began affirming that she deserved to be her own person. As that belief took hold, she was able to set firm limits about how much she would do for everyone and stick with them. She also began seriously to pursue her career. It wasn't easy, but the eventual bonus for Mindy and her family was that she began to feel more loving and giving as she gave up her slave role and became committed to having a life of her own.

It takes courage to retire Aunt Jemima and give ourselves permission to do what we choose to do rather than what we feel we have to do. As we gather the strength to give up living under the tyranny of our shoulds, we will feel more loving, and our giving will not be laced with resentment. We have the right to set limits and have lives of our own.

*I have the right to set limits
and the courage to do so.*

*Setting reasonable limits
makes me more loving to myself and my family.*

Teaching Others How to Treat Us

A BURDENSOME PROBLEM MANY OF US HAVE is the inability to accept our own worth. At some deep level we believe that we are not worthy of success, happiness, or supportive and loving relationships.

There is an old adage that "we teach people how to treat us." Do you teach those around you to treat you with respect or disrespect? When we believe we are unworthy, others treat us accordingly, but when we believe we are worthy of being treated well, we will accept nothing less. Inherently, we are worthy—our challenge is to know that and treat ourselves as we want others to treat us.

Recently a dear friend of mine discovered that for years she had been silently screaming at men, "How dare you treat me the way I feel about myself!" Now that she loves and accepts herself, others (even men) do, too.

You too can feel worthy of good treatment. Quietly close your eyes and recreate a time when you felt valued and accepted by yourself and others. If you can't think of an actual incident, make one up. Allow yourself to soak up the wonderful feeling of being treated well and with respect. Assure yourself that you deserve this excellent treatment. Let the feeling seep in to the very cells of your body. Revel in it.

Then, holding that mantle of good feeling around and through you, imagine a time when you were ill-treated. From a sense of deserving to be treated well, change the uncomfortable scene. Insist on acceptable behavior toward you. If the people in your visualization are not willing to treat you acceptably, walk away from the situation. Remove yourself. We all deserve to be treated well.

I deserve to be treated well.
I accept only acceptable behavior toward me.
I have the courage to teach people to treat me well.

Loving and Forgiving

*As selfishness and complaint pervert
and cloud the mind, so love with its joy
clears and sharpens the vision.*

—Helen Keller

NOTHING TAKES MORE COURAGE THAN TO OPEN OURSELVES TO the risks inherent in loving. To love is to be available and accessible to another—physically, emotionally, mentally, and spiritually. And, when we do that, aren't we vulnerable to the pain involved? If we have experienced ugly or hurtful circumstances, such as incest or emotional abandonment, under the guise of love, we are especially wary of love.

Loving (at least, giving to and caring for) others is one of the things women have had the courage to do best. But have we been able to love ourselves or allow others to love us? Feeling lovable springs from a healed inner child who feels she is worthy of love. Many of these pages will deal with nurturing the wounded little girl inside ourselves, so we can give and accept love in healthy ways.

As we have the courage to heal our past by looking back and inward—an often painful process—we can find ways to love ourselves and to truly love others. It is our right and responsibility, as well as our joy, to love and be loved.

Loving Our Inner Child

AT LEAST ONE ACTOR in our inner cast of characters is a wounded child who is at times shy, frightened, or in pain. She doesn't feel courageous or brave. Life seems awfully scary to her. Gently befriending our inner little girl and helping her feel safe in the world is taking a giant step toward emotional freedom and inner courage. For a healed child within creates an adult able to love and be loved.

It is often valuable to acknowledge our inner child with a comforting gift such as a teddy bear. Leigh has a soft, hand-sized teddy bear. At first she felt silly and embarrassed to admit that she, an intelligent grown woman, sometimes, during stressful periods in her life, wanted to hold her bear as she fell asleep. When she had the courage to allow her little girl the comfort she sought, she realized her bear symbolized "mother" to her since it had graced the bed of her own mother as she struggled with her final illness.

Take a few minutes and close your eyes. Imagine yourself in a beautiful setting where you feel comfortable and safe. Invite your little girl to join you. She may appear as a photograph you remember of yourself as a child, a symbolic representation of you, or you may only sense her presence. Anything you see is right. She may not trust you at first, so be gentle and take your time getting to know her. Talk to her, sit with her, listen to her, hold her. In the warmth of your love, acceptance, and attention, she will heal.

I have the courage to see my inner child as lovable.
My inner child is acceptable to me and to others.
I unconditionally love and accept
my inner little girl.

Deserving Love

UNTIL WE REALLY BELIEVE WE DESERVE TO BE LOVED, CHANCES ARE we will not draw healthy loving to us. Maybe, as a child, we were told we were bad; or maybe we assumed we were unacceptable from the treatment we received. Until about the age of seven, children feel everything that happens to them, or even around them, is their fault. As adults we rationally know that we were not unlovable as children, and that our parents and other important adults did the best they could considering their own wounds and limitations. But knowing we are lovable needs to register in our hearts as well as our minds.

Alice, well loved by her friends and family, always had the nagging feeling that someday everyone would realize they were mistaken about her and leave. She uncovered the reason for her feeling during a visualization when she vividly remembered a nun having her, for some minor infraction, fill a notebook page with, "I, Alice, am a bad girl." To help heal the label of "bad" which had plagued her all her life, Alice brought into her visualization a warm and kind mother figure who erased the original sentence and encouraged Alice to write, "I, Alice, am a good girl."

Because the concept of deserving love can be one of our most vulnerable areas—the home of some of our deepest fears—it takes a great deal of courage to look at our feelings of lovability. Therefore, we need to notice when we hear ourselves saying, "Oh well, maybe I don't deserve love," and become a loving and reassuring mother to our inner child, the kind of mother we all dreamed of having, always affectionate, available, and accepting. It is never too late to have a happy childhood. We can become loving parents to ourselves.

I am lovable.

I deserve to be loved.

Protecting Our Inner Child

MANY OF OUR ARGUMENTS, DISAGREEMENTS, AND OTHER PAINFUL encounters actually are between the wounded children inside each of us and not between the adults we appear to be. Once, when my partner and I were explaining the concept of inner children at a seminar, a woman participant began furiously waving at us for attention. She exclaimed, "You just saved my marriage! I don't hate all of my husband, I just hate and fear his mean inner little boy!"

When children are being unreasonable we create a "time-out" to allow them to vent their feelings alone. We can do this as adults too. Mary Beth, a client of mine, said, "It really hurts me when I have to listen to my husband tell me how stupid I am." She didn't have to; in fact it would have been better if she didn't. I encouraged her to recognize his little boy was having a temper tantrum when he berated her, and to leave the room until he cooled down and could talk on an adult level. Staying in the same room and allowing his inner little boy to harangue her hooked her wounded little girl and then the fur really flew between them.

If we find ourselves in a childish and destructive disagreement, we need to protect our own and the other person's inner child by venting away from each other and returning to the confrontation as adults. Conflict between wounded inner children never leads to a better understanding of one another or helps a relationship improve.

I love and respect my inner child.

I keep my inner child safe and protected.

I vent my feelings in a positive and loving way.

Asking to Be Nurtured

NO MATTER HOW OLD OR MATURE WE ARE, there are times when we need to be nurtured as if we were a child. Six months after my mother's death, I was frustrated and worried by some snags in the publishing of my first book. In order to meet a crucial deadline, I needed to call the typesetter. I was nine digits into the telephone number when I realized I was calling my mother's number. Crying and trembling, I understood my inner child was in despair and said to my husband, "I'm about four years old right now and I need my mommy. Would you please hold me?" He did, and my little girl sobbed out her frustration and grief.

When our inner child reaches out and asks for solace we must find someone who can respond lovingly. We need to be clear it is our inner child who needs the support. It was easier for my husband to hold and comfort a sobbing four year old than it would have been for him to console a near-hysterical adult. We know how to nurture kids, and we are not as afraid of their feelings as we might be of adults'.

Just because we live in an adult body doesn't mean we don't experience childlike feelings. Having the courage to ask for the nurturing we need helps us move through our feelings more quickly and effectively.

*I recognize my inner child's need
to reach out for comfort.*

*I give myself permission
to ask for comfort and solace.*

I love my needy inner child.

Creating a Safe Place

WE ALL NEED A REFUGE, A SAFE HARBOR IN WHICH TO REST AND BE replenished—a sanctuary created by the magical mystery of our imagination. Such a haven might be a beautiful green, sheltered garden where we meet, talk with, and are comforted by a wise and loving advisor. In our often fragmented days it is important for us to create such a sanctuary, a place from which to gather the courage, strength, and balance to creatively live our daily lives. An inner garden is often the most powerful solace we can find.

Close your eyes now and imagine yourself in a beautiful place. Feel yourself wrapped in the healing and protective embrace of someone who has only your best interest at heart. If no one you know comes to mind, create a loving person. Rest in her or his arms—a precious and valued child protected from all harm. Feel the caring, and carry the feeling throughout your day.

After we have established an inner retreat, we can return to it by merely remembering its beauty and peace. If there is a time in our day when we need reassurance or peace of mind, we can take a moment or two to revisit our sanctuary and be replenished in the safe embrace of our inner guardian.

I am loved and protected.

I am safe in the world.

*I use my wise imagination
to create a safe harbor for myself.*

Filling Ourselves First

WE KNOW IT IS IMPORTANT for our sense of well-being to give. In fact, there has been a scientific study which shows that the immune system responds positively when we help others and can be activated by merely watching a film about someone helping others.

But it is not healthy to give until we feel drained, used, and deprived. Such giving can be laced with hostility, resentment, anger, and the unspoken message: "Now you owe me!" This is not loving; this is bartering. We love best from a sense of overflow. When we are brimming with the energy that comes with having the courage to take care of ourselves first, our love and caring are freely given gifts, with nothing expected in return.

Our minds may tell us that filling ourselves first is an act of selfishness—it seems to go against society's dictum, particularly addressed to women, that it is more blessed to give than receive. It takes a tremendous amount of courage to realize that filling ourselves is essential. It takes even more courage to know how to do it, especially if we are out of the habit of thinking about nourishing ourselves.

To help move into the healthy pattern of filling yourself, ask yourself these questions and jot down the answers: What replenishes me so that I can love freely? What small step can I take today to allow time for myself to fill and refill?

We can do ourselves, and those we love, a favor by having the courage to fill our life's vase; by making a commitment to ourselves that, in order to be a free-flowing, clear fountain of love, we will fill ourselves first.

*I give myself permission
to fill my vase to overflowing.*

I freely love others from a sense of overflow.

It is loving for me to fill my own vase.

Loving from Overflow

BECAUSE TAKING TIME FOR OURSELVES is often a foreign idea, we need to have helpful reminders. When Verna turned fifty-nine, she decided it was time she had an adolescence. As the eldest daughter of an old-fashioned German family, she had been the designated mother's helper and servant. Leaving her parents' home, she married and had six children of her own. Circumstances such as illness, moves, and the usual responsibilities of a large family dictated that she put herself last.

Never thinking of herself was such an ingrained habit that even now, at age seventy-eight, she needs to give herself reminders to do so, such as paying her tuition in advance when she returned to school recently.

Many of us are in the same boat as Verna. We want to lighten our lives and nurture ourselves, but we don't know how. It helps to make a list of what fills us, gives us joy, and feels nurturing and healing. We need to check how much these people, activities, places, and attitudes we've listed are a part of our lives.

In order to absorb the feeling of receiving, sit quietly and close your eyes. Gently ask for the picture of a vase, which represents you, your life's vessel, to come into your mind's eye. If the picture you see is not one you like, change it until you have a vase that pleases you. Now visualize all of the fulfilling things you listed pouring into your vase. If good things refuse to fill your vase, stop and write in a journal any reasons you may feel unworthy. Gently, gently reassure yourself that you deserve to have what you want and need. And, remember, we love others best from our own overflow.

I open myself to receive all good things.

*I love others unconditionally
from the fullness of my own heart.*

Receiving from Others

LAURA, A YOUNG, BEAUTIFUL, AND BRAVE WOMAN I KNEW, recently died. For months before her death, women from her church volunteered their time working in her dress shop when she was too ill to be there. During that time Laura shared with them her feelings that her life had been good, and one of the best things about it was being able to fulfill her dream of having her own shop. In helping Laura, her friends gave her the gift of a dream realized, and she gave them the gift of feeling useful.

It is often tough for women to do, but there are times when it is healthy for us to allow others to nurture and care for us. Our lives are so much about serving others, being busy and useful, that we forget the value in balancing giving and receiving.

When we are sad, confused, depressed, or ill, it is important for us to allow ourselves to reach out and ask for what we want and need, even though to do so is scary. We will give those who care about us the precious gift of being able to help us, and give ourselves the gift of being supported when we need it. It is much easier for us to move through our feelings when we let go of the isolating belief that we should "go it alone." We need and deserve support.

I allow others to support me.

I deserve to be loved and supported.

*I have the courage to ask
for help and emotional support.*

Forgiving for Our Own Good

WE ALL HAVE PEOPLE IN OUR LIVES WE NEED TO FORGIVE—FOR OUR own good. None of us has gone through life without feeling hurt in some way or another. But to harbor resentment is to clog up our own flow of love and good feelings.

Forgiveness originally meant to "return good treatment for ill usage." Pamela discovered the importance of forgiveness when her husband left her for her best friend. Needless to say, she felt ill-used by them both. For a while she let feelings of hate and betrayal eat away at her, which caused her a great deal of mental anguish and didn't hurt either one of them a bit. As she had the courage to begin forgiving—first herself for her part in the marriage failure, and then her husband and friend—her whole life began to flow more freely. Her hurt and lack of forgiveness had blinded her to the love and support she did have from her children, family, and friends. As she forgave, Pamela was able to begin healing.

Lack of forgiveness clouds our ability to see the beauty in our lives and destroys our peace of mind. Carrying around hurt, disappointment, and resentment over the times we felt ill-used is like wearing several overcoats in Hawaii: hot, heavy, and hindering. Forgiving allows us to emotionally dress so that we can enjoy the balmy breezes.

Forgiveness is a process, and we need to allow ourselves to take one little step at a time. Our first courageous step is to be willing to give up our hurt—which often is terribly difficult—and focus on having a true willingness to forgive. If we only pretend we've forgiven someone because we know we should, it's like candying a rotten apple—it may look good on the outside but it's still rotten on the inside. We can activate our willingness to forgive and eventually actually be forgiving.

I am willing to be willing to forgive_____.

I am willing to forgive_____.

I forgive_____

Forgiving Ourselves

WE ARE ALL PERFECTLY HUMAN AND, THEREFORE, DO OR FEEL THINGS
we need to forgive ourselves for. Michelle, a young woman I worked
with, had been in a long-term, destructive, addictive love affair.
She ended that relationship but, as time went on, felt progres-
sively worse about herself and didn't have the courage to sustain
another relationship even though several young men had been
interested in her. She was miserable, paralyzed by confusion and
self-doubt. One day I asked her, "What would it be like for you if
you forgave yourself for your relationship with Kevin?" She looked
at me in total surprise and then broke into tears. Until that moment,
it had never occurred to her even to consider forgiving herself for
the mistake of choosing Kevin.

Unfortunately, Michelle's story is not that unique. Many of us
strive to adopt the Golden Rule toward others but often forget to
apply it to ourselves. We do unto ourselves as we would never
dream of doing unto others.

Although we have been encouraged to forgive others, statements such as, "Aren't you ashamed of yourself?" have given us the
belief that self-shame is fine but forgiving oneself is taboo. However, self-forgiveness is vital. Only in an atmosphere of forgiveness can we have the courage to be who we really are. When we
do not forgive ourselves for our mistakes, we encase ourselves in
an emotional straitjacket, afraid to risk, create, or feel.

We can start the forgiving process by making a list of what we
want to forgive ourselves for. Choose one thing and for a week,
insert it in the affirmation below. Then go through the rest of your
list in the same way. Forgiving ourselves makes us more open to
loving others.

I love and forgive myself as I would a dear friend.

I, totally and without reservation, forgive myself for_____.

Adding a Dash of Kindness

BECAUSE WE MAY SUSPECT THAT "NICE GALS FINISH LAST," IT CAN BE hard for us to open our hearts fully to others for fear of being hurt. It takes courage to add a dash of kindness to all of our encounters, especially if we have been wounded in the past. But if we can remember that nice wears well, and that our actions tend to draw similar reactions, it might be easier for us to believe being kind is safe.

We always have a choice about how to act, and when we choose to add a dash of kindness to our attitudes and actions, we bring joy and comfort not only to those on the receiving end but to ourselves as well. Giving a smile and a kind word usually elicits a similar response, and certainly lightens and brightens any encounter.

Authentic kindness (as opposed to play-acting "nice" because we are motivated by fear or guilt), a from-the-heart desire to reach out in love and compassion, is a reflection of who we really are—beings of love. Choosing to think, speak, and act with love—from the very center of ourselves—creates an ever-widening circle of love, kindness, and respect in our family, city, the world.

At times it may take every bit of courage we can muster to do so, but choosing to add a dash of kindness to our everyday activities is choosing to live in an attitude of love. As women, our highest calling is to extend and expand love. The best place to begin is with ourselves in our personal lives.

I express myself with love and kindness.

I have the courage to be nice, and I enjoy it.

I communicate who I really am—a being of love.

Loving Another's Inner Child

THERE ARE TIMES WHEN ANOTHER PERSON'S INNER CHILD treats us badly. It's very tempting to react from our own inner child and either become defensive or feel victimized. Since courage is partly having the willingness to do what we know is right even though it is difficult, it is courageous to choose to act lovingly when faced with someone's petulant inner child.

Penny's adult son was going through a period of blaming her for his unhappiness. After their initial conversation concerning his feelings about her failures as a mother, she was a wreck—alternately enraged and grief-stricken. She didn't sleep all night and the entire roof of her mouth became one big canker sore. Then she began to comfort and console her inner child, who was so ready to take the blame for her son's life, by reminding herself of all the good things she had said and done. With continual reassurance that she had done the best she could, she was eventually able to respond appropriately to her son's inner little boy.

When faced with raw, childish feelings in other people we are often tempted to say, "Oh, grow up!" But we need to look behind the outward behavior and know that their inner children are crying out. With that awareness we have a greater capacity to nurture the child inside.

If other people do not allow us to nurture them, we can at least feel compassion for their hurting child, rather than intimidated or guilt-ridden by their facades. It is easier to do this if, in our mind's eye, we see the adult we are dealing with as a two year old. Imagining an appealing baby in distress will help keep us from feeling intimidated and, therefore, allow us to feel safe enough to love.

I love, nurture, and respect
the inner child I see in others.

I listen to the inner child in myself and others.

Weaving a Safety Net

Woman must not depend upon the protection of man, but must be taught to protect herself.

—Susan Brownell Anthony

WOMEN ARE AMAZING. OUR LIVES ARE RARELY A STRAIGHT trajectory; instead we weave together an abundant existence from the varied and often unexpected occurrences that we encounter. Sociologists claim that women, because they are required to pay attention to many things at once, are *multiple-minded* and have great tolerance for interruption. Anyone who has juggled motherhood, career, education, myriad significant relationships, household management, and self-growth knows this to be true.

As we handle the woof and warp of our diverse lives, we need to be sure we weave strong safety nets for ourselves. When demands on us exceed our energy, we need to know how to support ourselves in finding the rejuvenation necessary to continue to thrive.

There are many ways—such as learning to understand and honor our needs, having realistic expectations, asking for help, and abolishing guilt—by which we can weave a supportive safety net for ourselves. I hope the following section provides you with strong fibers you can use to design a durable net that will comfort and support you when you need it.

Sharing Roots

ON A TRIP UP THE COAST of California and Oregon, I learned a valuable lesson about mutual support from the majestic redwood trees thriving there. Redwoods are inclusive beings—as they grow they incorporate into their basic structure objects around them, including rocks and other trees. Although redwoods have shallow roots they are noted for their strength and longevity because they share their roots with others. Each individual tree is invited into the whole and, in turn, helps support the entire group. This adaptation appears to have worked, for redwoods are among the oldest living things on earth.

Feminine energy is naturally inclusive and in order to survive and thrive we, too, need to learn to consciously share our roots with others, to ask for encouragement and support when we need it, and stand ready to give the same to those who come to us.

Eve, a single mother, was struggling with the idea of returning to graduate school. For weeks she kept her questions to herself for fear of appearing immature and needy. But when she finally risked talking to several women who had gone back to school, she was encouraged and supported by them. They included her in their root system. As a result of their discussions she began to feel clear about her next step. By having the courage to ask for help, Eve not only ended her confusion but found a support group that understood her circumstances.

In the process of creating support systems we need to be sure that those with whom we choose to share our feelings can be trusted to honor them. The best way to ascertain the trustworthiness of others is by monitoring your feelings as you talk to them. If you feel safe and understood, you have probably found a grove of like-minded redwoods.

By sharing our roots of compassion and support, we women, like the redwoods, create a safety net in which the whole is greater than the sum of its parts.

*I have the courage to ask for support
when I need it.*

*I am willing to support others
when they need my help.*

Editing Out Guilt

WOMEN ARE OFTEN PLAGUED BY FEELINGS OF GUILT, but I learned an interesting thing recently: guilt is a strictly English word. No other Germanic or Indo-European language has it. We need to follow the lead of these other cultures and edit the word guilt—and guilt feelings—out of our lives.

Feeling guilty drains our confidence and becomes a habit if we have been conditioned to be overly responsible for our own and others' behaviors and attitudes. Millie, a client in her mid-fifties, came to see me because she felt depressed most of the time. As we talked it became apparent that Millie was a Responsibility Sponge who sopped up everyone's messes. While discussing her unemployed thirty-year-old son, Millie sighed repeatedly and finally said, "I wonder where I failed?" When I asked her why it was her fault her son was not working, she looked at me with surprise and said, "Well, because I'm his mother."

Exploring Millie's background uncovered a family structure built on guilt and shame. Because of her conditioning, Millie got in the habit of assuming responsibility for everything and everyone around her. Since she, like the rest of us, had no real power over anyone's actions but her own, she felt discouraged and depressed. Millie decided to edit guilt out of her life using the following technique.

When you begin to experience guilt, ask yourself these questions: What have I really done to feel guilty about? (If there is something specific, decide whether you can rectify it, and if so, how.) Why am I responsible for this? Does this feeling and circumstance remind me of a pattern in my family? Do I want to keep feeling guilty about this?

If the answer to the last question is no, take a sheet of paper and write down what you feel guilty about. Now, with the biggest, reddest marker you can find, cross it out—delete it. If you find yourself still mired in guilt, remind yourself: *Guilt is a word and feeling I am editing out of my life!*

*I give myself permission to erase
guilt from my vocabulary and my life.*

*I have the courage to accept
responsibility appropriately.*

Coping Creatively

ALL OF US HAVE OUR OWN STYLE FOR COPING CREATIVELY. Some of us, like me, talk out our difficulties and, in the process of speaking the words, are able to work through the situation and resultant feelings. Others feel better able to sort through and arrive at solutions by mulling things over privately. Very often people in close relationships cope differently, and this can make each partner feel that she or he is doing it wrong. At such times, we need to remember that so long as we do so constructively, we each have the right to move through our problems in a way that is natural for us.

When Blair is confused or hurt, she needs to talk things through in order to gain a healthy perspective on her predicament, but her dear friend Marilyn is a solo-solution person. Blair used to chop holes in her personal safety net by comparing her style of coping with Marilyn's. She told herself that Marilyn was strong whereas she was a weak whiner, and that her friend must be smarter and healthier since she didn't seem to need help working things out. Most important, Blair was afraid Marilyn was tired of hearing her talk and was disgusted with her.

I suggested Blair start honoring her own style by talking out her feelings with Marilyn. When she did, Blair found that Marilyn accepted and enjoyed her need to talk—that Marilyn actually took into the privacy of her own process what she learned from their discussions and it often helped her heal more quickly.

It is important that we emotionally support ourselves by accepting and trusting our individual coping style, realizing that although there is no one right way, there is our way, and we need to honor it.

*I have confidence in my ability to cope
creatively with my challenges.*

*I recognize and honor my own style
of working things through.*

I have a right to my unique style of coping.

Pampering Is Permissible

When I ask women clients who seem drained what they do to pamper themselves, many of them respond uncomprehendingly, as though I've just spoken in a foreign language. To most of us, pampering brings to mind diapers or what we do for others. The idea of indulging ourselves is an alien concept; if it does occur, we avoid the idea because it smacks of being spoiled or selfish. After all, we've been taught to be givers rather than receivers.

Sarah, a workaholic, was married to a man who was still a little boy in terms of accepting responsibility at home. By the time she sought counseling, Sarah was, in her terms, "a raving, ranting bitch." Her bitchiness came from her anger at being the only adult in the family shouldering career, housework, and childcare. In the process of attempting to change her husband, Sarah had totally neglected herself and her emotional safety net was virtually nonexistent. Her nerves were frayed to the breaking point and she was lashing out in frustration.

I encouraged her to stop working so hard for him and start taking care of herself and then both of them might learn to believe that she was worth taking care of. It was very difficult for Sarah to change, but she began with the small step of allowing herself one hour a week just for the "luxury" of what she wanted to do.

Eventually she realized that she was not only more confident and rested but also a better parent, worker, and wife when she pampered herself a little each day. She is now able to care for herself in small ways, such as saying no when she feels like it, and large ways such as taking a trip she has set aside money for. Her children adapted quickly and have accepted and learned from their mother's ability to take care of herself. Even her husband is changing a little. Most important, Sarah is happier and healthier.

Weave a pampering pattern into your safety net. Make a list of ways in which you would like to pamper yourself, and then, starting with small steps, indulge yourself. You'll be better for it!

I have the courage to pamper myself.

I am worthy of receiving as well as giving.

*Pampering and taking care of myself is a
healthy thing to do.*

Softening Our Perfectionist

THE TROUBLE WITH BEING A PERFECTIONIST is that anything less than perfection displeases us. Since life is only sprinkled with perfect, fairy-dust moments while swamped with average-to-mediocre times, a perfectionist is only momentarily happy, which results in a pretty tedious life.

As for being a perfect person, having a perfect relationship, or doing all things perfectly, *there ain't no such thing*! And recognizing this increases our day-to-day happiness.

I used to have a part of myself that I named Ms. Perfection. When I visualized her, she was tall, bony, and ramrod straight with her hair pulled severely back into a knot. She wore half-glasses, a serviceable sweater with patches at the elbows, and white gloves with which she tested my ability to keep a sparkling house and personality. She made my life miserable until I learned to soften her by getting to know her and finding out what she needed from me.

As I became acquainted with Ms. Perfection, I became aware of her feeling that she was the only one of my inner cast of characters who acted responsibly. She believed she had to shoulder the adult stuff all alone and, therefore, had no choice but to be a rigid and harsh taskmaster. What she needed from me was a more consistent sense of responsibility and maturity. As I began working on that, she relaxed somewhat and became less judgmental.

Become aware of your perfectionist and ask yourself these questions: What does my perfectionist look like? Why does she act the way she does? What is she afraid of? What does she need from me? Am I willing to get to know this part of myself and help transform her by giving her what she needs, within reason?

Softening our perfectionist helps weave a safety net free from the gaping holes of impossible demands.

I have the right and responsibility to soften
my perfectionist.

I am worthwhile even though imperfect.

I loosen up and enjoy life's little imperfections.

Excusing Is Often Inexcusable

TO ENJOY INTIMATE AND AUTHENTIC RELATIONSHIPS, we must be able to understand and forgive ourselves and others. But we women sometimes confuse *excusing* with understanding and forgiving. Excusing, a codependent and childish habit, is the first cousin of denial. Excusing ourselves and others lets us off the hook by not addressing the consequences or responsibilities of our behavior. Alcoholic families frequently pivot around excuses.

Inherent in the process of excusing is our willingness to take responsibility for the actions of others. Continually excusing unacceptable actions does not create a climate that fosters growth and learning, in fact it can be an implied put-down. When we excuse the inexcusable, we are subtly saying that the person who is excused is not capable of right behavior.

On the other hand, understanding is a strong strand in our emotional safety net. Understanding our own and others' actions and attitudes provides an honest framework in which we can create an atmosphere of acceptance and forgiveness—an environment in which people and relationships can mature and thrive.

Understanding requires commitment, energy, and the willingness to be with ourselves and others in a heartfelt and open way. We need to make the effort to search for the causes and motives behind our own negative behaviors or attitudes and do what is necessary to heal them. Of course we can't do that for others, but we can tell them when their behavior is unacceptable to us and gently remove ourselves from their presence. Excusing may be initially more effortless than awareness, but it does not lead to intimacy, honesty, or authenticity.

I give up excusing my own and others' actions.
I want to understand myself and others.
I open myself to the ability to understand and forgive.

Gathering Ourselves Together

HAVE YOU EVER SAID, "I'M JUST BESIDE MYSELF TODAY!"? OUR LIVES ARE often like fall storms whipping branches and flinging the leaves of our concentration and contentment to the four winds, causing us to wonder how we can keep on keeping on. When we feel fragmented, we are actually beside ourselves energetically and need to gather ourselves back together again.

My wise mentor, Annabelle, taught me the following meditation that brings me immeasurable comfort when I feel frazzled and frayed. The purpose is to align our physical, emotional, and mental elements under our Higher Selves, which moves us from feeling beside ourselves to being integrated.

Close your eyes and visualize your physical, emotional, and mental selves. They can appear in any form or you may merely sense them. If you're feeling chaotic, they may appear to be moving quickly and, possibly, swirling out of control. After you see or sense these three aspects of yourself, envision your Higher Self— your spiritual part—above the other three. Softly say, "Together, together, together," three times—a total of nine *togethers*. As you repeat the words, picture the symbols for your physical, emotional, and mental aspects gathering together under, and finally into, your spiritual part. As you visualize, gently repeat the series of nine *togethers* until the parts merge and you begin to feel a sense of calm replacing the chaos.

Even though this exercise may seem simplistic, it speaks powerfully to our subconscious mind and allows us to gather our energy together, thereby naturally balancing and harmonizing our feelings. Standing in our own skins, rather than being "beside ourselves" allows us to move constructively through our busy lives, feeling *in sync*.

I have the power to replace chaos with calm.
I balance and harmonize the four aspects of my being.

Greeting the Stranger Who Is Myself

WOMEN HAVE ALWAYS KNOWN THE IMPORTANCE OF NETWORKING with other women, and now, because we travel the career path as well as the family path, we are also recognizing the value of networking within our chosen field. We go to meetings and join clubs for the express purpose of meeting people we can assist and be assisted by. But how many strangers are waiting inside of us for encouragement, acceptance, and support?

Kathleen was so sick of her job that she woke every Monday morning with a severe headache. Sometimes she burst into tears at the sound of the alarm. Even with messages as strong as these, she continued to work at the hated place. When I asked her why, she said she believed she would never find a superior job so she had better stay put. Another voice in her head told her she was darn lucky just to have work. And deeply buried was a barely audible, tiny little voice telling her she didn't deserve to be happy so it was fitting that she had a job that made her unhappy.

Courageously Kathleen began to greet these inner strangers. She found that many of the shoulds and have to's they spoke echoed what she had been taught as a young, single mother, having to work to support herself and her child. But the most important voice she became acquainted with was the tiny little girl inside who knew she didn't deserve happiness.

Kathleen made a commitment to comfort that little person who believed she was bad because she had never been able to please her critical and unloving mother. As her internal little girl became more secure and confident, Kathleen's sense of herself as a deserving person expanded. I am happy to say that she is now updating her resume, actively researching other work opportunities, and feeling vastly relieved.

Before she could successfully network in her workplace, Kathleen had to network within herself. Understanding and accepting the strangers within us provides an underlying strength to our emotional safety nets.

I listen to the voices of my inner selves.

I love and accept all of myself.

Growing a Tail

IT IS VERY IMPORTANT FOR US TO LEARN TO ASK FOR HELP AND BE willing to receive it, but it's even more important that we learn how to help ourselves. We're our constant companion and we know, better than anyone else, what is good for us and what we want and need.

The phrase, "God helps those who help themselves" is a sound and practical philosophy and one we would do well to follow. But I also love the lighter approach taken by the African proverb, "God will not drive flies away from a tailless cow." We all know tailless cows, people who always look outside of themselves for solutions and are adept at never taking responsibility for their own lives. Tiresome, aren't they!

During the trauma of the breakup of my first marriage, I regressed to a helpless state in which I, at first of necessity and then out of habit, hung on to my friends for support while consistently lamenting my situation. They were patiently willing to be there for me for quite a while, but finally my tailless state caused one friend to confront me about my seeming inability to help myself. Although the confrontation was extremely painful for me, it opened my eyes and I began to accept responsibility for my part in the breakup and learn ways to take charge of my own life. I grew a tail. At first it was neither a handsome nor effective tail, but it grew into a much stronger "fly foe" with practice.

Being able to rely on ourself as a loving helpmate is an integral part of weaving a powerful safety net. As we learn to consistently trust and support ourselves, our tails lengthen and, sometimes, some of the flies that have been persistently pestering us become discouraged and disappear altogether.

I am willing and able to help myself.

I take responsibility for my actions and reactions.

*I have a long, strong tail for brushing away
the annoying flies of life.*

Walking in Another's Shoes

EVERYONE HAS PEBBLES IN THEIR MOCCASINS. IN ORDER TO understand someone else we need to walk in her shoes—exchange our point of view for hers—for a little while. Doing this will allow us to let go of critical attitudes toward her. Of course, there are people with whom we will never feel compatible or want to cultivate a friendship, but we can coexist better by taking the time to try and understand their perspective.

Bertie's daughter-in-law, Tina, successfully tried to separate her from her son and granddaughter, and Bertie couldn't understand why. Being very conscious of mother-in-law jokes and pitfalls, she had tried to be caring but unobtrusive toward her son's family. She spent many fruitless hours lying awake fuming at Tina's actions, wondering how she could change her, until finally she exchanged her resistance for a desire to understand her better. Bertie made a choice to listen with her heart as well as her ears.

From the few fragments Tina was willing to share, Bertie pieced together an awareness of her daughter-in-law's fear of being controlled. Her new found awareness allowed Bertie to realize *she wasn't doing anything wrong* and to compassionately stop resisting Tina's choices. While it didn't change Tina's behavior, it did give Bertie much greater peace of mind.

Take a moment to imagine yourself in the symbolic shoes of someone with whom you have difficulty. Visualize how those shoes fit and feel. Do they pinch? Are they awkwardly large? Filled with grit? Allow yourself to really absorb what it must be like to walk in these particular moccasins. What do you now understand about this person?

Although we can't always alter circumstances, we can always transform how we perceive them. As we move from criticism and judgment to acceptance and understanding, our personal safety net is reinforced.

I take the time to listen to myself and others in order to better understand.

If I feel judgmental toward someone, I walk in their shoes for a moment.

Finding a Hand Up When We Bottom Out

THERE ARE TIMES IN EACH OF OUR LIVES WHEN IT FEELS AS THOUGH the pins have been kicked out from under us and we're absolutely sure we've bottomed out. Some of us feel guilty if we can't go it alone during such difficult times. But it's often healthier for us to ask for a hand up when we find ourselves in the pits. Trying to deal with things totally alone can magnify our pain and lead to feelings of depression and isolation.

Susan's husband was experiencing physical symptoms that doctors feared were indicative of a brain tumor. His way of coping was to deal with the physical pain moment by moment but not talk about the illness until he knew for sure what it was. He didn't want other people to know because "they would worry, and couldn't do anything anyway." Susan, who was beside herself with worry, felt more comforted when she was able to talk through her emotions with a select group of friends.

Although her husband objected to her sharing her fears at first, Susan convinced him that she had the right, and the need, to cope in her way just as he did in his. Only after she reached out to her friends did Susan feel able to climb out of her crater of despair and begin to draw on the strength she inherently possessed.

The story has a happy ending. Susan's husband's illness was treated successfully, and in spite of his original protests, she had the courage to comfort herself by honoring her need to reach out for solace and support.

If you are grieving or in pain, ask yourself if you are gritting your teeth and trying to handle the situation all by yourself when you might feel better reaching out. Or have you clenched your fists in anger and defiance at your misfortune and, consequently, could not accept a helping hand even if it were offered? If finding a hand up when you bottom out creates a secure and comforting safety net for you, give yourself permission to ask for help when you need it.

I honor what I want and need when I'm in crisis.

I am able to reach out to others for help.

I allow others to give me a hand up.

Acting As the Arms of God

ACTING AS THE ARMS OF GOD BY OPENING OURSELVES TO SERVICE for others is a beautiful pattern we women weave into our safety nets. Lending a hand and an empathetic ear can be a tremendous heart-lift not only to the person in need but also to the person serving. By opening ourselves to the needs of others we often find that we are "in the flow" where opportunities to be helpful present themselves in the most serendipitous ways.

One of my favorite stories about being given the opportunity to act as God's arms and help someone concerns Carole, a social worker. She and her husband were waiting for a table in a restaurant called Friends & Company when she noticed the hostess struggling with a phone call. Finally the hostess turned to the waiting customers and said frantically, "I've got a woman on the line who is hysterical and I just can't hang up on her. Is there anyone here who can help?"

Carole agreed to take the call and talked to the distraught woman for half an hour. She was able not only to calm the caller but also to offer practical advice about where she could turn for long-term help. The woman had called the restaurant because all she could think to do in her distressed state of mind was to look in the phone book under *Friend*.

When we commit ourselves to supporting and comforting ourselves by becoming our own good friend, a natural outcome will be the desire to recycle support by befriending others. The most important door we can open in our desire to be service-full is the one to our own hearts. Loving and accepting ourselves in a genuinely heart-felt way opens our hearts to others as well and invites God to use us as She sees fit.

*I support myself and, in turn, am happy
to support others.*

I open myself to being service-full.

I welcome opportunities to act as the arms of God.

Creating a Safe House

IN RECENT YEARS OUR SOCIETY HAS ESTABLISHED "SAFE HOUSES" WHERE battered women and children can find shelter. These secure havens are available only to the severely abused, however, so what about those of us who don't feel emotionally safe in our own homes or workplaces? If we are experiencing unacceptable behavior directed toward us by others, we need to set limits and clearly express what we will and will not tolerate so far as other people's attitudes and behavior go.

Although Sammi was highly respected in the business community, in her own home she experienced only resistance and rebellion from her kids and heckling and disrespect from her husband. Having come from an emotionally abusive family, Sammi believed their behavior must be her fault. She must not deserve to be treated well.

As we worked together, Sammi began to learn to respect herself and believe that she was worthy of better treatment. As a result of this healthier attitude, she set limits with her family that required they treat her with respect. She stopped waffling between protest and capitulation and stuck by the consequences she had decided on if they reverted to their old behavior. One of those consequences was allowing herself to check into a nearby motel for several days and let her husband fend for himself and take care of the kids. When her family realized she would accept only the new, respectful behaviors, they began to change.

Although this wasn't easy for Sammi and required painful, yet freeing, self-examination and commitment to change, she created a safe house for herself in the very home that had once felt like an enemy camp. Like Sammi, we have the right to live (and work) in a safe environment; therefore, we need to teach people how to treat us by setting realistic and respectful limits and sticking by them.

I deserve to live in a safe environment.

I have the courage to set limits and insist on respectful treatment.

I respect myself.

Making Our Own Choices

When you are in doubt, be still, and wait. When doubt no longer exists for you, then go forward with courage. So long as mists envelop you, be still; be still until the sunlight pours through and dispels the mists—as it surely will. Then act with courage.

—White Eagle

MAKING GOOD CHOICES IS ONE OF THE MOST POWERFUL ways we have to live courageously—to be who we really are. When we choose attitudes and actions that authentically express our true selves, we are inner-directed. If we feel the need to check with everyone but ourselves before making a decision or having an opinion, we are outer-directed. We women often have trouble with this because we've been led to believe that others are wiser than we are. But no one has the blueprint for our lives but us; so it is essential that we have the courage to make our own choices. Only then can we be sure that the life we are living truly exemplifies who we genuinely are. We need to gently persevere in believing that while not all of our choices will be perfect, if they're ours, they will be right for the process of our lives.

Cruising with High-Altitude Attitudes

WE HAVE THE CHOICE TO LIVE WITH HIGH-ALTITUDE ATTITUDES FILLED with optimism, enthusiasm, and excitement or to mope along with an Eeyore attitude of, "It's not much of a tail anyway. . ." Do our attitudes reflect the pure, clean, and heady atmosphere of high altitudes or are they murky and smog-congested? How we see life is up to each of us. If we don't like the view, we all can possess the courage and ability to change it.

At times Eeyore rides heavily on our shoulders, pessimistically warning us not to be too excited, too naive, or too enthusiastic. Not only are such low-rise attitudes depressing, they're boring. We can change our attitudes by becoming very aware of our thoughts and substituting positive thoughts for Eeyore thoughts. We choose our attitudes.

Imagine yourself on the top of a beautiful mountain. Feel the air, so clear it is like a zillion flawless diamonds reflecting the glistening sunlight. Bask in it. Take the magnificent view into your body— feel yourself expanding and lightening up. Say "Yes" to life! Feel yourself absorbing and exuding optimistic, powerful, and loving attitudes.

Choosing your attitudes, whether high or low, Pooh or Eeyore, determines whether you are happy or not. Have the courage to give yourself permission to live high, lightly, and with a resounding "Yes" in your heart. It is our choice, for we are the only guardians of our attitudes.

I am optimistic.
I say "Yes" to life.
I am light and I reflect light to others.

Uncovering What We Want

TRADITIONALLY WOMEN HAVE BEEN TAUGHT TO ACQUIESCE TO THE wants of others. They come first, whoever they are. Most of us were weaned on the idea that it is more blessed to give than to receive and it is difficult to break the pattern of denying our own wants. Going to the opposite extreme by adopting a selfishly militant attitude of "I'll do what I want and to hell with you!" doesn't get us the love and connection we want, even with ourselves. But there is a happy medium. A calm and centered knowledge that it is okay for us to have wants is essential to finding the balance.

If we have covered up our wants for a long time, we need to start gently by allowing ourselves to take a small-step approach to honoring our wants. For instance, Sylvia is a movie buff. She loves everything about going to the movies. Her husband is much more selective. For years she wouldn't go to the movies unless he wanted to go also. One day she garnered the courage to calmly and kindly decide it was okay for her to go, no matter what he wanted to do. That small movie-step Sylvia took years ago has grown into an innate knowing that she can make her own choices.

Making our own choices, and having the courage to overcome our them-first, me-maybe-never training brings freedom to our lives and our relationships. Our desires are valid and being aware of them is essential.

Sit quietly and think (or perhaps write) of a time when you deferred to someone else. Ask yourself what you wanted in that particular instance. Now imagine yourself making the choice gently but firmly to do what you wanted. If it feels uncomfortable, reassure yourself that you have the right to have wants and needs. Daily, practice asking yourself, "What is my choice? What do I want and need now?"

I have the right to make my own choices.
I have the right to have wants and needs.
I make choices easily.

Growing Up Emotionally

THOUGH IT'S OFTEN HARD FOR US TO GIVE UP THE OLD HABIT OF asking, "Mother, may I?" (or Father, or Husband, or Kids), we're living in an age when we have unprecedented opportunities to make our own decisions, create personal choices—to be ourselves. As we unravel our emotional dependencies, we learn no one can fill us with confidence, independence, and a sense of inner worth but ourselves, with the ever present help of God as we interpret Her/Him/It.

We may long to return to the fantasy that it's okay to be emotionally dependent, that some man will or should take care of us. For to really know the buck stops with ourselves is frightening. But it's also extremely freeing to realize we can be independent, confident, and in control of ourselves. We all are called upon to grow up, to assume responsibility for ourselves. As grownups we are better able to love independently, interdependently, and joyfully.

Having the courage to grow up emotionally, letting go of the myth that other people know better than we do, gives us a sense of freedom and self-confidence that nothing else can. Being grown up, in the finest sense of the term, is a powerful and secure way to live.

I am willing to grow up.

I have the courage to take responsibility for myself.

*I listen carefully to myself
and make informed decisions.*

Inquiring Within

SO MANY OF US ARE IN THE HABIT OF LOOKING "OUT THERE" FOR OUR answers, invalidating our own inner wisdom by assuming that, in some magical way, others must be wiser than we are—even about what is good for us. We become other-directed rather than self-directed. One of the biggest reasons for this behavior is that we are terrified of making mistakes. If we follow someone else's counsel, then it's his or her fault if things go wrong. But if we are to take charge of our own lives, we must have the courage to inquire within, find our own answers, and make our own mistakes.

So often my clients say, "I don't know" when I ask what they want or need in order to be able to make changes in their lives. To free them from their own inner pressure to give the perfect answer I ask, "Well, if you were to take a guess, what would it be?" Almost always they have an immediate and right-on "guess." We are our own best experts. We know what we should do. We are only afraid we don't know or afraid that our knowing will be wrong. It takes courage to listen to ourselves and act on what we hear.

We can learn to trust ourselves by inquiring within. To practice doing this, sit quietly, close your eyes, and for a minute focus your attention on your breathing. Gently visualize your inner wisdom as a graceful butterfly. Admire her beauty, and encourage your butterfly to sit on your shoulder and whisper her wisdom in your ear. Be still and listen. We do know what we want and need, and we can have the courage to accept the results and the rewards of inquiring within.

I am wise and capable.

I am my own best expert, my own authority about what is right for me.

I have the courage to listen to my inner wisdom.

Stopping Borrowed Trouble

BEING ABLE TO HANDLE ALMOST ANYTHING AS LONG AS WE TAKE IT one moment at a time is an idea we can accept intellectually. Yet how many of us gallop into tomorrow to see what trouble we can imagine there, or slip and slide back into yesterday to chew on its trouble? We need to make the choice to concentrate on what is on our plate today. Living in the now, borrowing trouble neither from the past nor the future, is one of healthiest choices we can make for assuring peace of mind.

I have a friend whose husband is critically ill and will, if he survives, have a long and tedious recovery. Whenever she slips into the past with regrets about what she might have done to help him avoid this illness, she quickly pulls herself into the now by saying, "I did the best I could. I will be even more careful in the future. I will just handle today."

When she begins to panic about the future, she allows herself to "wail like an Arab woman" and get it all out, then she says to herself, "I am thankful he is alive today. I will take care of myself today by going to aerobics, calling my kids, or going to a Japanese restaurant for sushi—whatever feels good. Right now, this minute, I'm okay." She is making the courageous and healthy choice to live in the present.

We all have the ability to choose to live in the moment, as my friend is doing. Broken down into minute-size or day-size pieces, even the most painful experiences can be handled with courage and grace.

I live in the present.

*I can courageously handle anything
as long as I take it one moment at a time.*

"This, too, shall pass."

Daring to Risk

GROWTH, LIKE ALL FORWARD MOVEMENT, REQUIRES THAT WE RISK, that we court the unexpected. Many of us avoid risking because we are afraid. Risking is scary, but it can also be exciting and energizing. Risking new ways of being can infuse us with enthusiasm and a sense of empowerment.

For many years the fact that her husband drank bothered Sadie, but she didn't dare confront him. Because he was neither an embarrassing nor abusive drinker, she rationalized that it was doing no harm. But it was. His drinking was making him unavailable to her and damaging her respect for him. Talking to trusted friends and going to Al-Anon helped her face her deepest fears. What if she confronted him with the fact that she couldn't live with his drinking anymore and he left or, even worse, ignored her important revelation, and she had to leave?

Courageously, she faced her fear of being alone and losing a man she cared for deeply and dared to risk confronting him. Because she had accepted the risk she was taking and practiced what she was going to say, she was able to talk to him in a loving and constructive manner. He has now stopped drinking and attends AA meetings regularly, and they are happier than they've ever been. For Sadie, daring to risk created a whole new life.

Risk may be scary, but it brings tremendous rewards, including self-esteem and freedom. We need to honor the fact that risk can be frightening, especially to our inner child, and gently, at our own pace, take the risks needed to enhance our lives.

I am willing to risk even when I am afraid.

I am proud of myself when I dare to risk.

*I empower myself by accepting risk
as a part of my life.*

Sidestepping Others' Negativity

WE SOMETIMES HAVE THE INCLINATION TO FEEL HURT AND ATTACKED by the actions or attitudes of other people. No matter how removed they are from us, we feel like their target. But we can tame the Target Dragon by learning not to take everything personally.

If the check-out clerk is brusque to us and our first reaction is "What did I do wrong?" or "Why doesn't she like me?" we feel vulnerable, as if we've been singled out because of who we are. A healing understanding to come to is, "I am not that powerful. People are not always responding to me, but to circumstances in their own lives." In the face of another's negativity, we can have the courage to reassure ourselves by affirming, "I am not responsible for this. I do not need to take it on."

When we no longer feel victimized or at fault, we can choose to send compassion and love to the crabby person. Even making up stories about them can be fun and ease our feelings. "Isn't it too bad she is suffering from constipation today." We can respond to others' negativity in a nonpersonal, light, and even loving way.

It is easier to avoid the effects of others' negativity when we question if an action or attitude is appropriately directed at us. If it isn't, we can choose to sidestep it and let it pass.

I sidestep others' negativity.

My peace of mind lies in not becoming defensive.

I protect myself in negative situations.

Selecting Positive People

ONE OF THE MOST IMPORTANT CHOICES WE MAKE IN OUR LIVES IS our selection of friends. A single rotten apple can ruin an entire barrel of good ones. Like those easily spoiled good apples, it's hard for us to maintain a positive attitude and high self-esteem when we're around negative people who undermine our sense of self. Avoiding negative people allows us to seek our highest level of being, unencumbered by the anchor of others' negativity.

Sometimes we live with negative people—what can we do then? First, we must become very aware of our limits. What comments and actions will we tolerate? Then we need to clearly state what those limits are and stand up for them. Usually, when we are firm about an issue, others will act as we have requested.

For example, Gail's husband, Joe, seemed to delight in putting her down by making fun of her in public and verbally abusing her in private. Her self-esteem was in the cellar, and she felt helpless—until she faced her fears about being single and truly decided she would rather live without Joe than be submerged under his pessimism. From a deep sense of conviction she told him that he needed to change or she was leaving. He's changing. It's not easy, but he knows she now feels good enough about herself not to accept his verbal put-downs and has the courage to leave if he doesn't clean up his act.

We can all choose who we relate to and greatly influence the way they treat us. It is so very important that we select positive people who lift our spirits and enhance our sense of well-being and that we do the same for them.

*I have the right to have relationships
that love and support me.*

I choose to be around people who lift my spirit.

Befriending Fear

Worry often gives a small thing a big shadow.

—Swedish proverb

ONE OF THE HARDEST TASKS IN MY LIFE IS TO TRY AND SEE FEAR as a positive, growth-producing emotion rather than something to be avoided at all costs. Although probably none of us is ever going to be thrilled by the prospect of feeling afraid, we all need to demystify and declaw our fear by increasing our capacity to examine it. Unexplored fear has the tendency to clasp us powerfully in its grasp, thereby limiting our ability to live fully and happily. On the other hand, when we have the courage to look fear in the face, we often find a treasure house of self-awareness and unrealized potential.

Befriending fear by realizing that it has much to teach us is an important step on our path toward becoming our authentic, confident selves. Although it's not an easy task, viewing fear as a teacher is necessary in order for us to keep it from becoming a demanding and overbearing taskmaster. As I face my own fears, I use encouragement, comfort, and support from various sources; my desire here is to share some of those with you.

Risking Business

As women leap deeper and deeper into the often choppy waters of the business world, we face a new breed of fear. Will we succeed or fail? Can we swim with the sharks without becoming one? Do we have what it takes to capitalize on our knowledge, market our wares, and stay afloat in a sea of black, not red, ink?

Many of us are afraid to take the risks that seeing our dreams to fruition would require. One of the best ways to transform our fears is to discover how realistic they are. Some of our fears are based on fact and result from personal experiences; many others, however, are remnants of old inadequacies and beliefs from the past.

Do you have a dream? Is there a business you have secretly longed to participate in? Are you avoiding an occupational risk because of fear? If you answered yes to any of these questions it will be helpful for you to take some quiet time and do the following exercise. Divide a sheet of paper into three columns labeled: "My Dream" or "What I Would Like to Do"; "Fears Inhibiting Me"; and "How I Can Transform These Fears." Quickly jot down answers that come to you under the appropriate headings.

Give yourself the gift of facing your fears, gleaning self-awareness from them, and encouraging yourself to risk in spite of them. And remember to turn to friends for support and encouragement. Comforted by the response you receive as well as your own successes, you can more easily trust your abilities and maintain the courage to continue risking.

I face my fears and learn from them.
I encourage myself to live my dreams.
I accept risk as a part of doing business.

Wisely Turning Tail

WE EACH HAVE INNER WISDOM THAT WE OFTEN DISREGARD. WE MAY instinctively know that a person or circumstance is not healthy for us, but still chide ourselves for foolishness or oversensitivity. In other words, we don't listen to the still, small voice inside us that knows. It's important that we begin paying attention to that voice, for it may be a bulletin from our wise self to turn tail and run.

Not heeding our interior oracle can cause us unnecessary pain. Anne, a young wife and mother, felt an innate dislike and distrust of another woman, Abbie, who was in her social crowd. But since everyone else in the group seemed to think Abbie was wonderful, Anne berated herself for feeling uncomfortable with her and made a special point of becoming her friend. As it turned out, Anne's instincts about Abbie were correct. Abbie, whose facade was unfailingly sweet, was a manipulative back-stabber and liar. Anne's failure to honor her intuition about Abbie and instead cultivate her "friendship" made it a double betrayal when Anne's husband walked out of her life and into Abbie's arms.

We constantly need to remind ourselves that we have an amazing wisdom—beyond our conscious perception—that often tries to warn us to stay away from certain people and experiences. Our job is to support ourselves by believing in and acting on these signals. Be alert to your inner cautions: sift through them, trusting that you know, deep down, what is good for you, and act on those that have external merit or persist internally. As Anne learned, it's sometimes very wise to honor our desire to turn tail and run.

I believe in my inner wisdom.

I honor my gut feelings by exploring them.

*I support myself by acting on my intuition
when appropriate.*

Building on Small Successes

FOCUSING ON OUR SUCCESSES, NO MATTER HOW SMALL, IS AN effective way to pare fear down to a manageable and realistic size. We all have everyday experiences that are successful and often have special and significant successes upon which we can also build. In order to have a happy and fulfilled life we need to focus on those "build-ups" rather than the "tear-downs." Yet it's so easy to habitually tear ourselves down by concentrating on our limitations rather than building on our successes.

For eighteen years Lynn was an active and involved at-home wife and mother. Her days were spent comforting and supporting her family, which included a hydrocephalic son who needed special attention. As the children grew, Lynn became increasingly restless and realized that she longed for a career as a computer troubleshooter.

Acknowledging her need to work outside the home in a challenging, male-dominated field created an eruption of fears in Lynn. She shared these fears with her women's group and, with their encouragement, began to work through her fears by taking one small step at a time and then building on that success. She experienced setbacks, of course, but congratulated herself on her success in weathering them and continued to persevere. In time, Lynn began believing and trusting in her abilities as a businesswoman.

Lynn is now the owner of a successful computer consulting business. Her road to success was paved with small steps, such as going to Adult Education classes, volunteering as a trainer for beginning computer students, working part-time, and doing small seminars for nominal fees. Her biggest accomplishments were surmounting her fear, overcoming barriers as they arose, and focusing on her modest successes one at a time.

Building a bridge of small successes can land us on the shore of our aspirations. What small, nonthreatening step can you take right now to help you befriend fear and build your own unique bridge?

I allow myself to take small steps toward my goals.

I accept and trust myself during both successful and difficult times.

Climbing the Peaks

I LIVE IN COLORADO, JUST AN HOUR FROM ROCKY MOUNTAIN
National Park. Being in the presence of those majestic, towering
peaks, peaceful valleys, and pristine alpine lakes always puts me
in a state of awed gratitude. Gratitude for both the beauty and the
ruggedness—the grandeur of the massive mountains, the delicate,
vulnerable beauty of the wild flowers, and the raw splendor of
uninhabitable stretches of frozen tundra.

Our lives are similar to this impressive landscape. We all experience peaks of excitement and exhilaration, valleys of assimila-
tion and rest, and chilling wastelands of depression and despair.
Climbing out of the pits and up the peaks is one of our main occu-
pations as human beings, and we need to trust that what is ultimately important is our overall progression. For often, to reach a
peak, we need to take a circuitous route that can include doubling
back and losing ground. At such times, the question to keep asking
is: Am I generally moving forward and upward?

Quietly close your eyes and visualize where you are in your
life today. Are you climbing a difficult slope toward the top of a
peak, calmly camped in a verdant valley, or struggling in a seemingly bottomless pit? Allow yourself to be wherever you are. You
are okay right here, right now. Very gently invite into your presence a supportive and encouraging Being who wants to assist you.
If you are content where you are, then relax and enjoy the presence
of your loving guide. If you would like to move out of the spot
you're in, ask the Being if it will help you make the change. Agree
to your Being's help and follow its guidance only if you feel totally
nurtured and accepted by it.

Life is a series of ups and downs, and it is our responsibility to comfort and protect ourselves during this inevitable process. We have what it takes to become peak-conscious rather than pit-bound.

I honor and accept life with all its peaks and valleys.

I stand in awe of the variety in my life.

I love myself even if I am in the pits.

Jarring the Kaleidoscope

IF OUR LIVES ARE LIKE KALEIDOSCOPES, MANY OF US SPEND A GREAT deal of time and energy attempting to create the perfect picture—colors and shapes all exactly as we like them—and then want to set the resultant work of art in a place of honor, never to be moved again. This is it. Now we've finally got it right. Then, Crash! Bang! Life has a habit of bumping into our carefully constructed masterpiece, jarring it into a totally different image.

For years Laura had struggled with her belief that it was her job to "fix" any crisis or difficult circumstance that came up in her family and at work. With a great deal of psychological savvy, Laura courageously became aware of her need to control situations in a futile attempt to keep her kaleidoscope in the pattern she thought best.

Little by little Laura began to release her need for control, accept what she couldn't change, and increase her peace of mind. She was proud of her new kaleidoscope pattern and was enjoying it immensely when breast cancer jarred her life. After first raging and resisting the cancer, Laura came to believe that the stress induced by her old need to control and correct all situations had so depressed her immune system that cancer was the result.

But Laura is a fast learner, and she has now not only licked cancer but has truly given up another big C word: control. Laura now consistently accepts and trusts the varying kaleidoscope patterns in her life and, most important, realizes that she is not responsible for everyone else's patterns. Awareness was her first, and most important, step toward her healing.

Are there areas in your life where you need to let go of control and allow your kaleidoscope fragments the freedom to dance to their own tune?

I realize that it is not my job to be in control of everyone and everything.

I accept and enjoy my life in its beauty and imperfection.

I am healthy, happy, and hopeful.

Questing for the Holy Male

CINDERELLA RAN AWAY FROM THE PRINCE FEARING THAT HE WOULD reject her if he knew who she really was, yet he searched for her and eventually took her away from a life of ashes and abuse to a happily-ever-after land. If we see the Cinderella myth as a metaphor for our inner process, we, too, often hightail it away from accepting our own masculine energy of dynamic creativity, leadership, and logical thinking, and then quest for an external male to carry these qualities for us.

This doesn't work. No one, not even the most wonderful man, can take the place of our own internal holy male. It is our scary, yet sacred, task to integrate both our feminine and masculine aspects into a balanced whole. If we are not aware of, or are frightened of, incorporating our masculine energy into our daily lives and instead look to a man for those qualities, we may have expectations that are unrealistically high or accept too little for fear of not being complete without him. In reality, the more we assimilate our male energy, the wiser we become in our selection of men as friends and mates.

Sit quietly and invite into your mind's eye a picture or symbol of your masculine self. If he is frightening, ask him why he feels the need to be threatening. If he is not a figure you can respect, ask him why he needs to appear weak. Allow yourself to get to know this part of yourself. What are his talents and fears, his dreams and aspirations? What qualities can he bring to your life? Befriend this important aspect of your being by asking him how he wants to be included in your daily life.

Incorporating our inner holy male and synthesizing our masculine and feminine selves brings us into a balance of doing and being—dynamic and magnetic energy—thereby creating a well-rounded whole.

I acknowledge and accept my masculine energy.

I explore any fears I have regarding my masculine aspects.

I am a well-rounded, multifaceted individual.

Living Our "Yes"

I SAW A NECKLACE, IN THE FORM OF A DOG TAG, WITH A SINGLE WORD, Yes!, engraved on it. What an enthusiastic affirmation of life! Sometimes fear, the great naysayer, gets in the way of our saying Yes to our dreams and talents and keeps us from reaching our highest potential.

Public speaking is one of my favorite ways to say Yes to living life to the fullest. I used to be absolutely terrified before giving a talk, but now I am usually only slightly nervous. Recently, however, I was catapulted back into almost paralyzing fear after seeing the publicity for an upcoming presentation. The little blurb on my talk outlined what people could hope to get from an evening with me, but I could not have delivered all they promised in a weekend workshop let alone the hour and a half I'd been allotted!

The Fear Serpent whispered convincingly, "They'll be disappointed. You'll be embarrassed." To still the voice, I did precisely the wrong thing—I ignored it. Because I was running away from my fear of failure, I resisted even preparing for the talk—a perfect way to set up the response I was dreading. Finally, at ten o'clock the night before my speech, I began to practice what I preach and explored my anxiety. Doing so helped me become aware of what I needed to do—take the fear out of my shadowy inner closet and share it with the audience. They, being fallible human beings also, could identify and empathize with me, and we ended up having a wonderful time learning from each other.

An excellent way to take fear out of overdrive is to strip it of secrecy: bring it out into the open. Crouching in darkness, fear hops in the driver's seat, but it begins to be transformed when brought into the light of awareness and acceptance.

In order to live our Yes!, we need to become aware of and accept our fear and then share it honestly where we will be gently accepted and supported.

*I am a strong and capable person even though
I have fears.*

*I accept and support myself especially when
I am feeling fearful.*

Overcoming Goal Blindness

IT IS VERY EASY IN OUR RUSH, RUSH WORLD TO BE SEDUCED INTO A state of goal blindness. By that I mean we become virtually blind to everything but the specific goal in front of us. When we're afflicted by such blindness, a gorgeous sunset, a friend's birthday, or even our own children's childhood, may come and go without our really paying attention. Reachable and realistic goals, interspersed with a few idealistic and hard-to-attain ones, are necessary and healthy; but being blinded by our goals—sacrificing spontaneity, fun, or family life for them—probably means we're being driven by some fear we need to uncover and heal.

Goal blindness leads to an imbalanced life. We are tyrannized by what "has to be done" and begin to dash through life as though it were a gourmet smorgasbord and we only had time for the bread. In order to lead a healthy life we need to balance inner and outer activities—stabilize the seesaw between doing and being, giving and receiving.

If you feel plagued by goal blindness, begin to free yourself by asking two questions: What fears are propelling me to work so compulsively? and, What is being sacrificed as I pursue this goal? As you answer, remember to do so in a loving and nonjudgmental way. You are doing the best you can, and are now in the process of making some new choices. That's a decision that deserves praise, not punishment. Next ask yourself this question: What small step am I willing to take right now to bring my life into better balance?

Goal blindness leads to rushing, and rushing is dehumanizing and injurious to all living beings, including ourselves. Although it's hard to break the habit of rushing blindly toward our goals, we can do it. With awareness, willingness, and commitment, we can learn to sample in a more leisurely fashion all the delicacies life has to offer.

I give myself permission to bite off only as much as I can comfortably digest.

I take one small step at a time toward rebalancing my life.

Standing by Our Core

THE WORD "COURAGE" COMES FROM A COMBINATION OF COR, WHICH in Latin means "heart," and *corage*, which is French for "the capacity to stand by our core." Standing by our core by having the courage to honor ourselves and value our needs is often difficult if we've been taught to put others first and ourselves second, if at all. It takes a great deal of heart to counter old beliefs about the appropriateness of standing up for ourselves.

Often we feel unsure about living in integrity with our core because we fear moving into a "me, me, me" mode of selfish behavior. The opposite is actually true. The more we honor ourselves by standing by our core beliefs and feelings, the more loving toward others we become.

When Meryl, a talented actress, left her husband, their friends were shocked because they had seemed like an ideal couple. In reality Meryl's husband was abusive, jealous, and demeaning in private. For years Meryl's best acting role was the one she played off stage—the happy and contented wife. Meryl feared she must be doing something wrong to elicit such behavior from her husband and she tried to change, but nothing worked.

Finally, after being painfully injured during one of her husband's outbursts, Meryl began believing that she didn't deserve such treatment. With the support of a therapist, she mustered the courage to face her fears and really value herself. In the process, she found that her capacity to love her daughter and others began to expand. The energy she had used protecting her family's secret by pretending all was well was now free to flow unchecked—even toward her former husband.

Having the heart to stand by our core requires that we pare away the layers of "he wants," "they expect," and "I should" in order to find the "I am," "I need," and "I can." By sensitively healing the fears causing us to betray our core, we can become accepting and supportive lovers to ourselves and others.

I have the right to honor who I am, what I need,
and what I can do.

I have the heart to love and support myself.

Remodeling the Rescuer

ALTHOUGH WOMEN ARE LEARNING TO STOP ACCEPTING RESPONSI-
bility for other people's feelings, we still seem prone to embrace
blame readily. In fact we often act like blame magnets, collecting
bits and pieces of negative mental pain and resentment, and believe
we are charged with the rescue of the senders. This is an extremely
uncomfortable way to live. In order to truly live in comfort with
ourselves, we need to make a concerted effort to renovate our
internal rescuer by permitting other people to rescue themselves.

Georgia remodeled her rescuer in one of the most difficult "fix
it" relationships to give up—that of mother and adult child. Georgia's daughter Carrie, a sensitive and artistic young woman, had a
series of semi-nervous breakdowns. The entire family went to
counseling, then Georgia and her husband financed Carrie's return
to college. When Carrie flunked out of school, her parents hired
her to work in their business, but she took advantage of the situation by consistently arriving late, if at all, and not doing the work
assigned.

Georgia agonized over Carrie's plight ("What have I done to
cause my daughter's weakness?") and made exceptions that she
wouldn't have made for a regular employee. The situation got
worse and worse. Now, although it is heartbreaking for her, Georgia is little by little allowing Carrie to deal with the consequences
of her actions. In order to have the courage not to race to the
rescue, but to let Carrie take responsibility for her own actions,
Georgia constantly reminds herself that she did the best she knew
how in parenting her child and that Carrie is now an adult in charge
of her own life.

Our need to rescue comes from both the desire to alleviate others' pain and a sense of blame or responsibility. Relieving pain, when it is possible, is good, but taking blame or responsibility is often a destructive pattern of behavior we learned early in our lives. We can transform that legacy by lovingly allowing others to rescue themselves in all appropriate times and ways.

I assume total responsibility for my own actions.

I allow others to take responsibility for their own lives.

Leaving the Mists of "Someday I'll"

WE ARE SURROUNDED BY INNUMERABLE OPPORTUNITIES. Possibilities for personal expansion, excitement, and happiness abound. Do we take advantage of them or do we crouch fearfully in the shadows saying, "Someday I'll learn to speak up for myself, clear up this relationship, write my book," etcetera?

Someday I'll does not honor the present, create a positive future or support our self-esteem. Hiding in the mists of *Someday I'll* may appear safe but usually leaves us filled with regret for things left undone and unsaid.

But what if we're frightened about doing or being something new and have relegated the desired change to "maybe tomorrow"? We need to transform our fear by having the courage to look at it and heal it. We can start by asking ourselves what is keeping us stuck.

Mary, a former teacher, had been struggling with what career path to follow as she entered her fifties. For two years she investigated different options but nothing held her attention for very long. Mary began to explore her fears in depth and discovered that she had been a very demanding taskmaster with herself in all areas of her life, including her teaching—everything had to be perfect or it was unacceptable. She came to understand that she was frightened to start a new vocation for fear she would once more beat herself up with unrealistic requirements.

Mary's commitment to let go of perfectionism assisted her in her decision to enter the seminary. At the age of fifty-two, she's left the mists of *Someday I'll*, in part by assuring herself that she will pursue the ministry only "as long as it continues to feel right!" By adopting a tolerant and flexible attitude such as this, Mary is free to follow her calling.

If you have a dream languishing in the mists of *Someday I'll*, gently encourage yourself to examine any fears that may be keeping you from realizing your dream right now. In the warmth of loving self-support, our fears can dissipate and we are empowered to confidently follow our heart's lead.

I make decisions easily.

I allow myself to follow my heart's lead.

I do it now.

Transforming Inner Tyrants

WE ALL HAVE AN INNER CAST OF CHARACTERS THAT I CALL SUB-personalities. Often these internal family members remain strangers to us, neither accepted nor synthesized into our lives. Sub-personalities are formed or de-formed around our beliefs and assumptions and, if unrecognized, can cause us to act and feel in ways that are detrimental to our well-being.

We can integrate the estranged parts of ourselves by becoming aware of their fears, wants, and needs. Each of our sub-personalities has, at its core, a positive quality. Acceptance allows that quality to manifest itself in our lives.

Sit quietly with your eyes closed and gently invite your inner cast members to appear, as though on a stage. They may emerge as people, symbols, animals, or just as a sense or feeling. Without judgment observe them from a distance. What do they look like? How do they feel? Are they comfortable or uncomfortable, happy or sad, calm or angry? And very important, how do you feel toward them?

Choose the sub-personality about whom you feel the most accepting and begin to get acquainted with it. For a few moments, just be together, sensing how you feel about each other. Is there trust and respect, love and acceptance? What quality does this inner family member have that you would like expressed more in your life? Ask it what it wants and needs from you. Are you willing to give that?

Now do the same exercise with the sub-personality who most disturbs you. Remember that each aspect of ourselves, no matter how vile it may appear or act, has at its center a positive quality. When liberated from the dark cellar of our subconscious into the light of our acceptance, it can become a creative spiritual force within us.

Tenderly befriending and supporting all our cast members allows them to transform from inner tyrants into trusted friends.

All parts of me are good at their center.

I heal and transform my wounded inner selves
by loving and accepting them.

Disappearing into Availability

OUT OF A DESIRE TO DO THE RIGHT THING OR A FEAR OF REJECTION, we can make ourselves so available to those we love that we become invisible to them. We disappear as a person and become merely an anonymous constant to be taken for granted. Amy Tan, author of *The Joy Luck Club*, wrote, "My Amah loved me so much that I no longer saw her except as a convenience there to serve me."

If we feel lost in a labyrinth of other people's demands and desires, we need to look beneath our facade of helpfulness and unearth any unhealthy fears or beliefs we have that are allowing us to be taken for granted.

To help yourself discover areas where you disappear into availability, write a list of circumstances in which you feel used or taken for granted. For each separate entry ask yourself why you continue to act in a way that results in your feeling invisible and undervalued.

If your answer begins something like, "I'm afraid that . . . ," question your fear: Is it realistic? Is this an old fear from childhood that has no validity in your current life? Who, in your inner cast of characters, is experiencing the fear? What do they need from you to help alleviate their fear? If your fear is realistic, what is the worst thing that could happen if you changed your behavior? Do you have the maturity and wisdom to support yourself emotionally if the worst scenario was realized? Although it's not easy to change patterns of over-accommodating behavior, we can do so by assuring ourselves that we have the right and the need to be available to ourselves as well, which, in turn, will make us less resentful of and more loving toward others. Healthy availability enhances relationships, but self-denial and overindulgence destroys them. It's necessary for our well-being—and the good of humanity—that we are available to others, but it is essential that we honor and support ourselves in the process.

I am available to others in a way that enhances their life and mine.

I deserve to be visible and valued.

Taming and Transforming Dragons

When we face our fears and let ourselves know our connection to the power that is in us and beyond us, we learn courage.

—Anne Wilson Schaef

OFTEN WE FEEL WE HAVE TERRIFYING, FIRE-BREATHING DRAGONS zealously keeping us from the path to self-esteem and happiness. A great majority of these beasts, hatching and gaining strength in the dark caves of our subconscious, are generated by fear. Fear is the single most limiting factor in our lives. It binds us to hurts of the past and barricades our path to a fulfilled future.

It takes tremendous courage to extricate ourselves from the clutches of our fear-filled and limiting inner dragons, but when we fail to look at them directly, they gain strength. Growing quietly away from the light, they eventually rise up threateningly to demand our attention.

Freedom comes from having the courage to know that fear is not to be avoided, but faced, lived through, and learned from. Every time we face a fear and walk into the middle of it with support from others, a little bit is dissipated. Continually having the courage to face the internal dragons of our fears frees us from living reactively and gives us the opportunity to be who we truly are.

Facing the Dragons of Fear

ROBERT FROST ONCE SAID, "THE BEST WAY OUT IS THROUGH" AND nowhere is that more true than with fears. In fact, the only way out is through. When we run away from fear, it ends up running us! Unhealed fear acts as a fog, shrouding from view our myriad possibilities. Fear also is a magnet, drawing to us that which we fear.

Angie's fear that her husband would leave her was so deep she could not leave the room at night without him. If she wanted to go to sleep before he was ready for bed, she curled up at his feet. Her husband was devoted to her, and she could not understand why she was so afraid of being abandoned. She was terrified to look for the origin of her seemingly groundless fear, and her terror was justified. Wisely, she asked a therapist to be with her on her journey toward healing.

As she had the courage to look inside, Angie remembered an extremely abusive relationship with her father culminating in his disappearance when she was seven. As a little girl, she feared her father treated her badly because she was bad. When he left, she believed he had done so merely to be away from her. Consequently, as an adult, she carried inside her a deeply embedded fear that she was not worthy of love—especially from men.

Thankfully, most of our fears have less traumatic beginnings than Angie's, but if we are grappling with debilitating fears or fears we cannot understand, it is important we have the courage to explore them with a qualified person whom we trust and with whom we feel safe.

When examining fears we feel capable of handling alone, it is helpful to sit quietly and think of something or someone we fear. Then ask ourselves, "Why do I feel scared?" "What is the worst thing that could happen if I faced this fear and moved through it?" "Could I survive my imagined consequence?" Often our answer will be yes, if we have the courage to take it one day, one hour, one minute at a time.

I am willing to face my fear of_____.

I have the courage to face my fear of_____.

Rejecting the Rejection Dragon

ALL OF US ARE AFRAID OF REJECTION. WE ARE MUCH MORE susceptible to this fear when we feel we are unlovable. And how often do we allow ourselves to acknowledge how lovable we really are?

Marie lives in constant fear that her lover will reject her even though he assures her he loves her deeply. I asked her why she harbored this fear and her rather sheepish answer was, "Well, I don't think I'm very lovable." Hopefully, Marie will be able to change her feelings about herself. If she doesn't, she is likely to begin acting unlovable in order to stay congruent with her belief system. Without being able to view herself as lovable, she may actually drive her lover away.

When we feel unlovable, it is the wounded little girl in us who is hurting—the little girl inside who was either told or told herself that she was not okay, not worthy of being loved. Having the courage to love our own little girl is the primary step toward allowing others to find us lovable.

In order to help heal your wounded inner child, close your eyes and imagine yourself in a beautiful, protected environment. Visualize your little girl in this safe place with you. Become as open and loving toward her as you can. Reassure her that she is lovable and acceptable by telling her all of the things you like about her.

If you can't feel supportive and accepting of her, invite into the scene a compassionate mother figure who can love her unconditionally, and allow that woman to hold and comfort her. Realizing and accepting the fact that we are worthy of love is the best way for us to tame the Rejection Dragon.

I see myself through loving and accepting eyes.
I love myself and allow others to love me also.

Knowing We Can

I GREW UP WITH A FRIEND WHO WAS BORN WITH ONE ARM MISSING from the elbow down. Before every adventure we were planning, I would ask her, "Do you think you'll be able to do this?" Her answer was almost always a resounding, "If you can do it, I can too." And she did.

Most of our limitations are self-imposed. When we know we can do or be something, we generally can. But knowing is not the same as wishful thinking. Wishful thinking is passive; knowing includes having the courage to find our way over, around, or through obstacles we find blocking our path.

"I can't" is one of the most debilitating beliefs we hold. Imagine that something we want badly is on a raft one hundred yards from shore and all we need to do is swim out and claim it. On the sand are swim-fins and a ten-pound bowling ball attached to an ankle chain. We can choose either of these to help us get to the raft. No contest: the fins. But many of us choose the bowling ball and chain of "I can't" and wonder why we struggle and sink on the way to getting what we want.

What we think is totally within our control. It is wise for us to choose swim-fin thoughts to help glide us toward our goals. We can either sink with "I can't" or swim with "I can."

I have the courage to know that I can.

I am capable and creative.

I help myself achieve my goals by knowing
I can surmount any obstacles in my path.

Sacking the Bag Lady

LURKING IN MANY OF OUR MINDS IS THE FEAR THAT WE WILL END UP an impoverished bag lady. This fear can exist whether we are young or old, married or single, wealthy or poor. Often this fear comes from a sense of deprivation, the belief that life is like a pie and there is only a limited amount of good to go around.

Laurie is a wealthy woman but because she lives in fear of losing her money, she never enjoys what she has now—today. On the other hand, Malia is a fifty-year-old widow with very little money who feels abundantly blessed by her children, grandchildren, and friends. She feels secure that she will always have what she needs and has an attitude of thankfulness. When she needs it, money appears out of "nowhere" to get her through.

It is important that we have the courage to face and exorcise the ghost of deprivation when it haunts us. We can do so by ferreting out the underlying beliefs that create our fear and replacing them with a belief in abundance. While examining our fear, we may discover an underlying belief like, "I never have enough" or "I don't deserve to have enough."

Self-talk like this reinforces our fears. Becoming aware of this self-talk gives us the opportunity to change it to empowering statements such as, "I am thankful for what I have, and I trust I will always have enough." When we truly believe there is plenty, we draw to us that which we need.

Life is not like a pie, but rather like a never-ending spring—constantly flowing—renewing and replenishing itself. We can live with a spirit of joy and abundance when we change our beliefs to ones of unlimited supply.

Life loves giving to me.
I trust that I will always have enough.
I am thankful for what I have.

Owning Our Own Excellence

OFTEN IT'S HARD FOR US TO LET GO OF OUTDATED AND ERRONEOUS self concepts and see how really excellent we have become. I know that's a tough one for me. On the eve of sending my first book to the printer, I received one of my old college transcripts from my former husband. My prepublishing nerves were already raw, so what I saw in that transcript—some C's in English—sent me scurrying to my bag of tricks to help dislodge the Fear-of-Failure dragon that was sitting on my shoulder smirking and wiping his feet on my confidence.

Wanting to recapture a modicum of confidence, I visualized the young woman I was in college and reassured her that she was intelligent and capable even though her English grades were average. Then I began to focus on all of the education and life experience I had to offer through my courage and willingness to write honestly about my own fears and transformations. I brought into my mind's eye memories of people who had thanked me for helping them. I then listed talents and abilities for which I felt grateful. Slowly I began to internalize the feeling I had much to offer no matter what grades I had received twentysomething years ago.

With a simple change of focus—from concentrating on fear to accentuating ability—we learn to own our own excellence. If our self-esteem needs an update, we can make a list of our excellent qualities and even have the courage to ask our family and friends what they find excellent about us. It is okay to believe in our own excellence.

I accentuate my abilities.

*I own my own excellence by concentrating
on the good in myself.*

I have the courage to believe in myself.

Refocusing Our Binoculars

ALL TOO OFTEN WE WOMEN ARE OVERLY SELF-CRITICAL. WE BELIEVE that it is more acceptable for us to maximize our shortcomings and minimize our strengths. We have learned it is not feminine to toot our own horns.

Self-critical people see their mistakes leaping before them festooned with neon lights, while their triumphs wither from lack of attention. They look at their real or imagined shortcomings through powerful binoculars and look at their good points and successes, if at all, through the wrong end of the binoculars. Failures loom large and ominous, and successes look like specks on the horizon, mere accidents of nature.

It is courageous to refocus our binoculars, to give ourselves permission to move beyond self-critical thought patterns and realize what fantastic people we are. We can learn to "SEE": Savor Excellence Everyday by becoming an honest and appreciative mirror for ourselves. We choose to focus on the good in ourselves, learning from the things we wish we'd done better without allowing ourselves to magnify them out of proportion.

Making a list of things we like and admire about ourselves and tucking it in our purse is a good way to help us reinforce change. If we notice ourselves focusing on the negatives about ourselves, we can take out our list, read it, and then add another positive to it. Maybe our positive will be that we noticed when our binoculars needed refocusing—that's a great habit breaker.

I focus on my positive attributes.
I like and admire myself.

Healing through Feeling

SOMETIMES WE FIND OURSELVES SUPPRESSING OR DENYING OUR feelings for fear others will not allow, understand, or accept them if they are voiced. Only through honoring and acknowledging what we really feel can we heal and move on. Yet we women are often called "overemotional" and "PMS" to discourage us from sharing, or even knowing, our true feelings.

In the face of such attitudes, it takes deep courage to allow ourselves to explore and express our true feelings. We can help ourselves resist the seductive Dragon of Denial by reminding ourselves frequently that we each have a right and a responsibility to experience our feelings.

Our physical bodies offer good examples of "healing through feeling." When we get the measles or chicken pox, for example, we feel sick for a while and then we become immune to that particular disease. Our bodies intuitively know that to move through the illness is to move toward healing.

The same wisdom is valid for our emotional dis-ease. As we move through our feelings, express them, learn from them, and allow them to heal, we become free of them.

*I have the courage to know and experience
my true feelings.*

I have a right to my feelings, whatever they are.

I express my feelings constructively.

Rechoosing How We Want To Be

A BIG PART OF OUR ADULT WORK IS RECHOOSING HOW WE WANT TO be. Most of us didn't have a perfect childhood. However, if we are still caught in a web of negative behaviors and patterns from childhood, we can free ourselves.

Until Janice was sixty-two years old, she always felt defensive and guilty when she visited her mother. I asked her two questions that helped her free herself from the web of old reactions. "How old are you when you visit your mother?" After a thoughtful moment, she replied, "A rebellious twelve!" My next question was, "How old do you want to be?" She wanted to be sixty-two years old and sure of herself.

Knowing that the simple act of passing through her mother's door dropped 50 years from her age and catapulted her into the uncomfortable pattern of old responses allowed Janice to remind her inner twelve year old she was now an adult and had no need to rebel against her mom. It worked. By the time her mother died three years later, their relationship was clear and comfortable.

When we notice ourselves acting in ways we dislike, we can stop and consciously choose how we would like to act or respond in that instance. We are not chained to the past; we have the power right now to rechoose how we want to be.

I can see old patterns when they arise
and free myself from them.

I appreciate the good things about my childhood and let go of the pain.

I have the power to be who I want to be.

Uprooting "Rootless" Fears

WE MAY DECIDE THERE IS NOTHING TO DO BUT LIVE WITH A FEAR that seems irrational to us and grit our teeth in an attempt to bear with it. But there is a healthier way for us to proceed if we are experiencing fears that seem rootless, out of proportion to the apparent cause, or have no "logical" basis.

We need to give ourselves a priceless gift: time to explore confusing fears. The unknown can be so frightening that confronting fears, the origins of which we can only guess, takes tremendous courage. But it is also freeing, for only when fears are brought to conscious awareness will we be able to discover how to heal them. As long as fears remain hidden we are held helplessly in their grasp.

Since the root of our fears most often lies in childhood, we can expect to experience childlike feelings while rediscovering them. Seeking emotional support at such times is not dependence; it is wisdom. Taking the risk and having the courage to examine our seemingly rootless fears is best done in a protected and supportive environment. Before we begin to explore our inner demons, we need to find a person or a group with whom we feel safe, people we can trust implicitly with our vulnerability. It is okay to reach out and ask for assistance. In fact, it's often essential.

*I invite into my life the perfect people
to support and nurture me.*

I have the courage to explore my fears.

*I create a safe and protected environment
in which to transform my fears.*

Escaping the Depression Pit

DEPRESSION IS THE CLASSIC DISEASE OF WOMEN. DEPRESSION IS LIKE a fog that settles over us, limiting our ability to see what we're really feeling. But when we change the first two letters of the word, we have expression rather than depression. If we don't express what we're feeling—what's bugging us—in a constructive, healing manner, very often the result is depression: the way women weep without tears.

Often depression is really anger we've turned back on ourselves. If we are feeling depressed, we need to check and see if, deeper, what we're really feeling is anger. Anger is natural—it's how we tell ourselves, "Something isn't right here." But too often, women are taught anger is bad.

Betty gave in to anger once as a pre-teenager. Walking into her closet one day, she slipped in a little puddle her sister had left on the floor. She swore and her mother heard her. Her punishment for expressing her anger was being forbidden to attend a dance she had looked forward to, and her mother wouldn't speak to her for the rest of the day. Through this and other similar experiences, Betty learned to invert her anger to avoid rejection and punishment.

We are only really depressed when we're so foggy that we're not aware of our feelings. If we are aware of them and working them out, even if they are angry or sad, we are in the very healthy process of healing. Having the courage to overcome our conditioning about anger, and learning to express it constructively, are two of our sturdiest ladders out of the depression pit.

*I am a good person
even though I sometimes feel angry.*

*I give my inner child permission
to have and express her feelings.*

*I have the courage to work through
my anger constructively.*

Chirping Up by Looking Up

FEEL LOW SOMETIMES? CAN'T SEEM TO DRAG ONE FOOT AFTER THE other? The weight of the world perched leadenly on your shoulders? We can chirp up by using a simple body language technique. Because our mind/body connection is extremely potent, we have more power than we imagine to elevate the "down" feelings we experience.

If we're depressed, our body will read our mind and translate the feeling into posture—slumped shoulders, head forward, eyes cast down, draggy and droopy gait. The exciting news is that our mind can also read our body. We have absolute control over how we hold our bodies. We cannot sustain depression if our eyes are looking up, our body is standing straight, and our walk is jaunty.

As an experiment, assume a position that is depressed and down. Hang your head and let your tummy sag out. Check your feelings. Do they match your posture? Now get excited! Sit, or better yet, stand up tall—stretch to your full height. Hold your head up proudly and look up. How does that feel?

Our minds and bodies, good servants to each other, listen for each other's commands. We can give ourselves a lift by looking up, straightening up, feeling up.

I help myself feel up
by looking and straightening up.

I am an up, excited, and energetic woman.

Feeling Worthwhile

ON OCCASION, ALL OF US FEEL WORTHLESS (WORTH LESS THAN THE next person). As a young and neophyte therapist I was shocked when an older and infinitely wiser (I thought) colleague told me she was in therapy. "What do you have to work on?" I asked. "Oh," she said, "feelings of personal worth. You know, same old thing we all work on."

Her remark underscored the idea that, even though we might wish it weren't true, our work on ourselves is never ending. We are always called upon to have the courage to continue on our path toward greater and deeper feelings of self-worth.

We are worthwhile just because we are alive. However, feeling worthwhile is an inside job. It is our task to assure ourselves of our worth by the way we treat and talk to ourselves. Other people can be very complimentary and supportive, but if we secretly know we're worthless, their words slide off as if we were teflon-coated.

Mentally check your self-talk. Does it enhance feelings of self-worth? Do you treat yourself as if you were valuable and precious? Do you make yourself and your well-being a priority?

If not, close your eyes and mentally step back from yourself. How do you feel toward "you" as you view yourself from a slight distance? If you feel supportive and loving, great. Tell "you" how much you appreciate her and how worthwhile she is. If you do not feel supportive and loving, bring in to the scene a wonderful woman (real or imagined) who does love and support you and have her validate your worth. Soak in her validation and claim it as your own.

I am valuable and worthwhile.
I treat myself in a manner that fosters self-worth.

Embracing No-Fault Living

I always see the good that is in people and leave the bad to Him who made mankind and knows how to round off the corners.

—*Goethe's mother*

SO MANY RELATIONSHIPS FLOUNDER ON THE ROCKS OF disapproval and blame. In order to enjoy comfortable, companionable, and mutually supportive relationships, we need to embrace the art of no-fault living. This doesn't mean that we become a patsy and allow others to walk all over us, but it does mean that we learn to curb our criticism of others and insist they do the same toward us.

No-fault living includes accepting and supporting ourselves, our friends, and our loved ones. No-fault living builds up confidence; it means never putting down or making fun of ourselves or others. When there are uncomfortable issues to confront, we discuss them in a way that leads to understanding and solutions but doesn't cast blame.

Everyone is imperfect, and having that fact pointed out to us in a critical fashion (and is there really any other way to do it?) decreases our chances of expanding and enhancing our capabilities. In the face of censure, we become fearful of doing or saying anything and learn to walk on eggshells. Criticism dams the flow of good feelings, whereas encouragement and support strengthen our ability to become the best person we are capable of being.

Owning Our Own Projections

ONE OF THE BEST WAYS TO ENSURE FULFILLING RELATIONSHIPS IS TO be confident of who we are and have an honest and supportive relationship with ourselves. Why is this so important? Because, to the extent that we don't know ourselves or are blind to our vulnerabilities and prejudices, we will unknowingly project those shortcomings onto our relationships with others.

For instance, if we berate and judge ourselves when we make a mistake, we're likely to think that other people are also judging us when, in fact, they may be completely unaware of the mistake.

We need to become aware when we say things such as "He won't let me" or "They don't listen" if we are actually projecting an internal feeling that "I don't trust myself to do that" or "I don't listen to myself because I fear I don't have anything of value to contribute." If we are projecting, it is our internal scripts, and the feelings creating those scripts, that need editing and revision.

It is impossible to ask "them" to treat us in ways we do not yet treat ourselves. Therefore, we need to consciously realize when we are projecting our unfinished business onto others so that we can reclaim those projections and heal the erroneous self-concepts that created them.

We are the authors of our lives, and we can write new, healthy scripts that cast us as lovable and deserving women. As a result, we're more likely to be appreciated by those around us and our relationships consequently will be enhanced.

I am willing to acknowledge my own projections.

I have the courage to heal emotional wounds that keep me from having good relationships.

I love and support myself.

Throwing Out the Gauntlet

THROWING DOWN THE GAUNTLET IS AN INVITATION TO A DUEL; IT'S issuing a challenge—in effect, sticking our chins out and saying, "I dare you!" While this kind of attitude may be apropos for sports or other contests, it is not conducive to developing harmonious personal relationships. Mutually supportive partners do not issue challenges through the gauntlets of blame or competition—both loud calls to dueling. Instead, they are committed to eliminating blame and playing fair. Cooperation, not challenge, leads to satisfying relationships.

If we find ourselves having an aggressive attitude in a relationship, we need to throw the gauntlet *out* into the trash, not *down* in front of the other person. When we're dedicated to learning to live supportively, we choose to communicate in ways that allow us to complement rather than compete with each other, ways that foster harmony rather than dissent.

Sit quietly, close your eyes, and allow to effortlessly arise in your mind a relationship in which you are locking horns with someone, a situation that is a challenge and frustration to you. View this predicament nonjudgmentally. What gauntlet have you thrown down? What blame are you casting? What challenge have you been unwilling to accept?

In your mind's eye, gently step back from the scene and picture it as though from your higher self. Ponder how you might eliminate blame and bridge the troublesome impasse by approaching it with a goal toward understanding and cooperation rather than convincing and winning.

Since it's difficult to remain open and vulnerable when faced with an adversary, intimacy is usually the casualty of a thrown-down gauntlet. The old proverb about catching more bees with honey is true: with supportive attitudes and a desire to understand, we can "catch" more sweetness in our lives.

I find myself and others blameless.

I communicate nonjudgmentally with the goal of understanding.

Figuring Out Who's Fighting

SO MANY OF OUR FEELINGS STEM FROM OLD FEARS WE KEEP BURIED in the trunk of our past. When these feelings surface, we may act irrationally, baffling and scaring those—including ourselves—who experience the brunt of our emotions. Often, out of frustration and bewilderment, fights erupt. In order to sort things out, we need to figure out who's fighting.

Lana and her fiancé, Mitchell, were having a terrible argument. In the face of her seemingly irrational fear of getting married, he had withdrawn into an icy silence. As a result, she felt abandoned and screamed at him that she was canceling the wedding. In response he disgustedly left the house. Sobbing, she called me. After listening to her story, I asked her who was feeling abandoned. In a moment, she thoughtfully said, "Oh! I think it's me at about three years old."

As a three-year-old, Lana had good reason to fear abandonment; now her adult self was acting out that old fear in response to the marriage commitment she was about to make. She told Mitchell who it was in her inner cast of characters that was fearful, and he was able to realize that he wasn't intimidated by Lana's inner three-year-old. But, *his* insecure little boy had been terrified by what he saw as a raging adult rejecting him.

The insights Mitchell and Lana gleaned from their premarital confrontation led them to make a commitment to help each other figure out "who's fighting" when seemingly groundless feelings arise in the future. With a renewed appreciation for each other's sensitivity and vulnerability, and an awareness that they could comfort and support their own and each other's scared inner child, they were married as scheduled.

If baffling feelings grab you by the guts and fights threaten to erupt as a result, ask yourself who is in the grip of the emotion. You'll probably come face-to-face with an old fear. The bearer of that fear needs and deserves your acceptance and reassurance.

*I support myself emotionally by figuring out who,
inside, is the bearer of scary feelings.*

I comfort and support my needy inner child.

Jousting with Our Inner Knight

ALTHOUGH WE'RE ALL ENDOWED WITH BOTH FEMININE AND masculine tendencies and talents, in western society the logical and linear masculine is seen as the more valuable. Unconsciously we often evaluate ourselves by society's standards and end up confused about what is worthwhile and appropriate within us. Our undervalued femininity, the bearer of intuition, wisdom, and empathy, feels the need to joust for place and power with our masculine inner knight, whose talents include getting the job done, empowerment, and motivation.

We need to integrate, not separate, the masculine and feminine aspects of our being. Through accepting and trusting both, we can help our inner knight free himself from his emotional armor as well as rescue our damsel from the dragon of victimization and weakness she has been subjected to by the narrow views of society. Synthesizing our varying, but equally valuable, feminine and masculine attributes and proficiencies creates balance, harmony, and wholeness.

Take a few silent minutes to effortlessly visualize your inner knight and lady. Are they able to work harmoniously with each other? If so, congratulate them and joyfully observe their dance. If not, encourage them to begin communicating with each other. What are their fears? What do they want and need from each other? How can they move toward sincere and lasting cooperation and mutual support? Don't expect miracles at first. Simply becoming aware of our feminine and masculine aspects and opening a dialogue between them is very healing.

The quest for mutually supportive relationships extends not only to those with whom we live, but also to those who live within us. By becoming acquainted with and accepting our differing parts, we can stop internal civil wars and learn to live as a productive, positive, and balanced whole person.

I love and admire both my feminine and masculine attributes.

I accept all parts of myself.

Flying toward the Flame

HAVE YOU EVER FELT AS THOUGH YOUR MIND WERE FILLED WITH frantic moths fluttering around the flame of an insult or hurt? Try as we might to tame them, sometimes our thoughts insist on flying in and around the fire of our pain, and we end up feeling scorched by anger, guilt, or some other equally disturbing emotion.

During a fight with my husband in which I couldn't seem to get across to him why I was so angry, my thoughts were darting around in a frenzy. The drums they gyrated to were filled with fault-finding chants—*he should, I shouldn't,* and *if only!* I couldn't sleep and, because we were in a hotel room, I couldn't go off by myself to do some calming meditation. I became more and more resentful as I lay there, exhausted, endlessly recounting my woes.

It wasn't until the very early morning hours that I began having the image of my thoughts as kamikaze moths determinedly flying toward the flame of my anger. With that valuable impression, I was able to begin calming my moths and cooling the flame, at least enough to allow me to drop off to sleep.

If you find yourself moth-minded, try this meditation. Close your eyes and conjure up a picture of your thoughts as moths. Allow yourself to see the flame of your resentment or anger and watch as your thoughts circle dangerously around it. Purposefully fan the flame and encourage it to burn even brighter. Watch as the flame licks and dances. Then very slowly and without judgment begin to deprive it of oxygen by putting something over it to snuff it out. As the flame quietly ceases to burn, gently gather up the moths and release them in a beautiful meadow filled with sweet-smelling flowers.

When we find our thoughts obsessively drawn into the flame of emotional pain, we need to consciously redirect them to a calming image or affirmation that encourages peace of mind. One of the most comforting statements I have used during such times is, "I can do all things through God who strengthens me."

I can change my thoughts.

I let go of anger and resentment easily.

Removing Thorns

IF WE GET A THORN IN OUR FINGER, OUR NATURAL RESPONSE IS TO pull it out—to eliminate the source of pain. Yet how many of us allow emotional thorns to embed themselves in us without ever acknowledging that we have the right to pull them out? Emotional thorns run the gamut from a relationship that is detrimental to our self-esteem to regret or guilt over something we did or that was done to us. Left unattended, emotional thorns can fester and acutely infect our attitudes.

Sherry, whose mother is an alcoholic, is a sad example of the damaging effects of unhealed emotional thorns. When Sherry was a child she mothered her mother and didn't receive the nurturance she needed and deserved. As an adult Sherry continued to care for her mom, but her feelings toward her turned to resentment and bitterness.

Although externally she did all the right things, internally the emotional thorn of her regret over her childhood experiences grew more and more poisonous to her daily life. Wisely, she sought counseling and learned to gently mother her inner child in ways that satisfied her longing. She plucked from her mind the primary sentences in her regret-litany and replaced them with self-valuing affirmations.

She also learned to set boundaries. Sherry's therapist once told her, "There is a statement in the Bible that goes something like this, 'You have the right to remove yourself from those who are vexations to your spirit.'" Today, she limits her caregiving of her mother to only that which she can do without resentment. She now supports herself when she is in need and encourages herself to remember that she has the right to remove emotional thorns.

Intuitively we know who and what is good for us. If we listen to ourselves with appreciation and trust our wisdom, rather than create judgments about our frailties, we'll know when it is healthy for us to remove our emotional thorns, and we'll give ourselves permission to do so.

I encourage myself to heal.

I have the courage to remove painful emotional thorns.

Tilting at Disrespect

IN ORDER TO FEEL ACCEPTED AND SUPPORTED BY OUR ENVIRONMENT, self-respect and the respect of others is essential. But many of us have not required others to treat us with respect and we often disrespect ourselves. To change this pattern, we need to cultivate a *pinball-machine* mentality and, when treated rudely or when overly jostled by demanding people including ourselves, go *tilt* and refuse to cooperate.

The first and most important step we can take toward a life characterized by respectfulness is to tilt at any disrespect we show ourselves. The habit of self-*dis*respect is not an easy one to break, but we can do it. Gently and without recrimination, we need to observe our self-talk for signs of devaluing and blaming; then we can return to a supportive, no-fault attitude toward ourselves by creating self-talk that underscores and bolsters our self-respect. For instance, when we hear our inner voice saying something disrespectful such as "I can't do *anything* right," we need to stop and say, "Whoops, that's not true!" and alter the statement to a considerate one.

The same principle is true when we begin insisting on respect from others as well. If at work you are given responsibility without power or are expected to jump at the first scream from overly demanding and spoiled children or adults at home, ask yourself if you feel respected. If the answer is no, *tilt!* Since it's true that we teach people how to treat us, refusing to be treated shabbily is essential in earning the respect of others.

Although at first the people around us may be surprised by and resistant to our new call for respect, generally we'll ultimately receive the treatment we persist in requesting.

I deserve to be respected.

I respect myself.

I expect and insist that others treat me with respect.

Calming the Inner Sea

SO MUCH OF THE TURMOIL IN OUR LIVES IS THE RESULT OF OUR NEED to be right. Often we hold on to a grudge because we righteously know we're *right!* And maybe we are. But does that stubborn insistence that the other person acknowledge we are right add to our happiness or build a dam between us and him or her? Dr. Gerald Jampolsky, author of *Love Is Letting Go of Fear*, has a wonderful little statement that he tries to live by: *Would I rather be right or would I rather be happy?* I know which I choose—what about you?

It's difficult to give up the idea of being right because until we have an unshakable sense of our own worth, much of our security and self-esteem comes from believing we are right. But living with the attitude of *They better see it my way* or *I have to be right* leads to a stormy life filled with resentment.

I once had a couple in my therapy practice who had a heated argument over the habits of great white sharks. Each was sure they were right about certain details, and the more they tried to convince the other, the angrier they became. Finally, one turned to the other with a rueful grin and said, "Who the hell cares about sharks, anyway!" With that acknowledgment, they both began to laugh and the boiling emotional sea was calmed.

Calming our inner seas by deciding we would rather be happy than right doesn't mean that we acquiesce to others or relinquish our beliefs. It just means that we choose to let go of unimportant things that we have a stubborn tendency to gnaw on, terrier-like.

As Emmett Fox, the founder of Religious Science, says, "When you hold a resentment, you are bound to that person with a cosmic link." We want and need to be *connected* to others in supportive, loving ways, not bound to them by resentment, resistance, and the need to be right.

I calm my inner sea by choosing to be happy.

I allow myself to float free of resentment.

*I love and accept myself when I am right
and when I am not.*

Dumping Dependence

IF WE CONTINUOUSLY LOOK TO OTHERS FOR OUR SENSE OF SAFETY, rely on them to make us feel worthwhile, and bank on their loving us to make us feel lovable, we are putting responsibility for the quality of our lives in someone else's hands. This makes us overly dependent, which is bad news for all concerned. In healthy relationships there is mutual *inter*dependence, but we need to dump dependence that is detrimental to our self-esteem and well-being.

Do we depend upon ourselves first for support, encouragement, and acceptance, or do we habitually cast about outside of ourselves, depending on others to provide these things for us? Of course there are times when it is natural and wise to seek reassurance from others; however, we need to be our own biggest boosters. We need a constant friend *inside* ourselves whom we can count on to encourage and nurture us no matter what the circumstance.

Allow your eyes to close gently and become as comfortable as you can. Imagine yourself in a beautiful, serene, and safe place. Quietly sink into the ambiance of this special location. Invite a presence that symbolizes your inner security to come and join you. It may appear as a person or as a symbol, such as an animal or a white light—any symbol is fine so long as you feel loved by it and in tune with it. Soak in the sensation of being protected by, and at one with, your inner security. Ask it how you can become better acquainted with it and be able to call on it confidently when you need it. Thank it for appearing to you, and let it know how much you appreciate it.

As we learn to have confidence in our inherent strength and accept it as an integral part of our higher selves, we will be able to dump overdependence on others and make room for mutually supportive interdependence.

I trust myself.

I am my own best expert.

I support myself unconditionally.

Cultivating Compassionate Detachment

DO YOU EVER FIND YOURSELF ACTING LIKE AN EMOTIONAL VACUUM cleaner, swooping into the corners of other people's pain and sucking it up as if it were your own? Although we may think this is the loving thing to do, it's not. It is important that we empathize—understand and comprehend another's feelings—but it is equally important that we try not to sympathize—allow others' feelings to affect us in a similar fashion. Sympathizing does not alleviate the other person's distress and it renders us less capable of being supportive, because we become swept away by our own feelings instead of able to concentrate on their experience.

An effective way to support others who are in pain is to cultivate compassionate detachment. Compassionate detachment asks that we feel deeply for another person, and understand the extent of her pain, without immersing ourselves in it or assuming responsibility to solve it or *make it better*. Compassionately paying attention to someone's distress is more constructive than attempting to *fix it*. Each person must find his or her own solutions, but being supported and encouraged along the way is a wonderful gift.

When I'm feeling pain that I can't understand, or if I realize I've vacuumed up someone else's pain, I find the following prayer very helpful: *Mother/Father God, if this is not my pain, I ask that it be taken to its perfect, right place and there be transformed and transmuted into the perfect, right energy. If it is my own pain, I ask for an understanding of its source. Thank You.*

Cultivating compassionate detachment frees us from "sympathy pains" and allows us to be truly involved with others by providing empathetic comfort, encouragement, and support.

*I release all feelings that are not my own to their
perfect conclusion.*

I am a compassionate and empathetic person.

I care but do not carry.

Knitting the Raveled Sleeve

SLEEP, AS SHAKESPEARE SAID, KNITS UP THE RAVELED SLEEVE OF CARE. And who among us does not go to bed some nights with substantially raveled sleeves? We need our sleep because it replenishes all of our resources— emotional, physical, mental, and spiritual.

But just as an anorexic deprives her body of food, we sometimes starve ourselves of rest by attempting to sleep in an environment where we are overpowered by our partner's cover stealing, restlessness, or snoring.

Diane struggled out of bed each morning bleary-eyed and resentful, having spent yet another night unsuccessfully trying to block out the sound of her husband's snoring. By the time morning arrived, her nerves were frayed, her creativity dwindled, and her disposition soured. She almost hated him—the unwitting instrument of her torturous sleeplessness. When talking to Diane about her dilemma, I encouraged her to support herself by finding a comfortable place where she could sleep peacefully. With some guilt and trepidation, she mustered the courage to move into another bedroom.

Just recently she told me that the move had saved her marriage. Watching Diane and her husband affectionately holding hands and laughing with one another, I could see the new relationship they had forged out of her willingness to take care of herself.

If our sleep vibrations do not mix and match well with our bed partner, this may sometimes mean we need a bedroom of our own. The sleep-on-the-couch cliché does not have to be a derogatory comment on the state of our relationship; rather it can mean that we have supported ourselves by creating a comfortable sanctuary, a feminine haven where we can get our much needed rest and knit up our raveled sleeve of care, undisturbed.

Sleeping well during the night means we are more likely to have an accepting and supportive attitude toward the people we meet during the day.

I sleep easily and peacefully.

I have the right to sleep in a comfortable, restful place.

Leaving Shame and Guilt Behind

THE PERSON WE MOST OFTEN STAIN WITH FEELINGS OF SHAME AND guilt is ourself, and much of our guilt and shame comes from believing we have failed in some way or other. Maybe we "should" have been more successful, or "shouldn't" have had an abortion, or "should" have been able to stop his drinking. Some of us can go on forever "should-ing" ourselves.

Mary Pickford, the actress, had a bit of insight on this subject I think we would be wise to adopt. "If you have made mistakes . . . there is always another chance for you. . . . You may have a fresh start any moment you choose, for this thing we call 'failure' is not the falling down, but the staying down." Very few of us stay down for long.

Sadie and Ashley, mother and daughter, were talking about their past. Ashley told her mom that she would tell her more about what she was struggling with but didn't want Sadie to feel guilty. Sadie wisely, and with hard-earned self-love, said, "I'm over that. I see we were in the same circumstances, but I didn't cause them. If I'd had the power or the awareness, I would have changed the situation. I didn't have either, and I did the best I could." Don't we *all*!

Make a list of your seeming failures—the "shoulds" you think you need to feel shameful and guilty about. Ask yourself if you did the best you knew how at the time; if so, think of a symbolic way to release these feelings. For instance, a friend of mine gave me a jar labeled "Shoulds and Oughts." Periodically, I take out the little scraps of paper on which I have put my shame and guilt and burn them as a symbol of letting go and moving on.

Yesterday is irretrievable and tomorrow is unknown. We have done the best we could, and now it's time for us to forgive ourselves for our seeming failures, congratulate ourselves for getting up after falling down, and then leave remorse behind us.

I forgive myself for what I see as my past failures.

I deserve to be free of shame and guilt.

Accepting Our Former Selves

AS WE JOURNEY THROUGH LIFE, WE PLAY MANY PARTS; INDEED WE seem to be entirely different people at various ages. Some of those old selves may cause us to cringe with embarrassment and regret now, but a commitment to gain confidence and comfort ourselves necessitates moving back through the pages of our history and embracing those selves.

I had an experience that brought home to me how easily we hoard judgments against our earlier selves. Several years ago my former husband told me he had never been sexually attracted to me. He explained that he had always been captivated by small, petite brunettes. That's not me!

I was pained by his revelation but, more than that, relieved. I had always blamed my young married self totally for the failure of the marriage (after all, a woman worth her salt can keep a man, right?). But now I knew that I couldn't have changed my physical appearance.

In meditation, I invited the Sue I was in my twenties—uptight, French rolled, and unhappy—to come into my presence. Having always been a failure in my eyes, she came warily. Greeting her in a new, more understanding way, I assured her that she had done all she could, that the marriage failure was neither hers nor her first husband's fault—they were too young and unable to be honest about what their needs were. Holding my young, former self in maternal, accepting arms, I asked her to forgive me for the blame I'd heaped on her all these years. She softened and seemed to become more confident as we both shed tears of reconciliation.

Take a quiet time to move back through the years and allow the image of an earlier self, one who needs your acceptance, to come into your mind. See the two of you enveloped in a clear and cleansing white light. Allow the light to flow through and around you both, healing any separation and bonding you together in love. From the wisdom of your current age, reach out and welcome that younger you into your heart.

I accept my former selves.

I become a loving mother to my younger selves who need my forgiveness.

Developing Healthy Selfishness

THE FEAR OF APPEARING (OH, HORRORS!) SELFISH CAN LEAD US TO give ourselves away until we are exhausted and drained absolutely dry. A dry well has nothing to offer to others. Cultivating selfishness can be a virtue that activates an ever-flowing spring of goodness from which we can share liberally with others.

It really is true that we do unto others as we do unto ourselves. Those who first love themselves are able to love others more genuinely. As we honor our own wants and needs, we can do the same for others. Those who truly love themselves—as opposed to being self-centered or self-absorbed—can trust, accept, and support others from a place of *I give freely* rather than *I need, therefore I give in hope of some return.*

Sit quietly and tune in to your breathing. Allow it to move as it will. After watching your breath for a few moments, encourage it to deepen. Take in new air from a loving universe and release used air to an accepting universe. See yourself, symbolically, as a vase—a vessel for sacred water. How full are you? If you are full to overflowing, you have much to offer the world. If you are less than full, your task is to *selfishly* fill your vessel. As you inhale, see your vase filling with crystalline water; as you exhale, let go of your old ideas about being selfish. Breathe and fill. Breathe and release.

Make a list of the things you would like to do for yourself but haven't because you thought it would be too selfish. If you do these things, will your life be richer? Will you be happier? Will you have more peace of mind? Will you be able to let go of some resentment? Will you feel more supportive of yourself? If you answered yes to any of these questions, your life and your relationships will benefit from the infusion of a little selfishness. So give yourself permission to be selfish!

*I have the right and the responsibility
to take care of myself.*

*I lift my vessel to Life and allow it
to fill to overflowing.*

I cultivate the virtue of healthy selfishness.

Ringing True

We should not pretend to understand the world only by the intellect; we apprehend it just as much by feeling.

—Carl Jung

WE FREQUENTLY CATEGORIZE OUR FEELINGS AS GOOD OR bad, acceptable or unacceptable, and attempt to include only the good and acceptable ones in our lives. This usually doesn't work; because feelings are very often illogical and originate from old beliefs and experiences, they are not so easily managed.

Imagine that you have a galvanized tub—the apple-bobbing kind—filled with water and red and white Ping Pong balls. Let's pretend that someone has told you the red balls are bad and you need to keep them out of sight, below the surface of the water. How can you do it with just two hands? The only way I have come up with is to cut a piece of wood the size of the tub and hold down *all* of the balls—white and red alike. The same principle applies to our feelings. When we feel we have to submerge our "unacceptable" (by whose standards, I wonder?) feelings, we, of necessity, suppress others also. We become numb. Our lives lose their brilliance and excitement and we get confused about who we really are.

By becoming aware of our feelings, accepting them, and expressing them creatively and constructively, we free ourselves to be fully human.

Embracing Our Imperfections

WE GRANT OURSELVES AN IMMEASURABLE AMOUNT OF FREEDOM ONCE we stop chastising ourselves because of our imperfections. Part of being human is to be less than perfect. This does not mean that we don't strive to be the best that we can be, but it does mean that we commit to being tolerant and supportive self-observers. With an encouraging inner perspective, we have a better chance of transforming our imperfections than with a hostile and judgmental attitude toward ourselves.

Many years ago when I was first learning the importance of loving myself, I met a man who taught me a very important shortcut to embracing imperfection. Cecil was a former Baptist minister whose father and grandfather had also been ministers. He described his family as a long line of perfect guilt carriers. In order to free himself from his belief that he had to be perfect, he regularly and good-humoredly shouted, "I made a mistake, so sue me!"

I took his motto as my own, and for years, when a less-than-perfect action or reaction overwhelmed me with feelings of shame, I would privately roar, "I made a mistake, so sue me!" Eventually, I began believing that I didn't have to be totally perfect all the time.

If we have been dedicated perfectionists for years, it will be difficult to embrace our imperfections, but it is possible. Not only can we learn to accept our peccadillos, but we can also begin to see them (providing they are relatively harmless) as rather likeable parts of our uniqueness.

Take a moment now to run a little movie in your mind with you and one of your self-proclaimed imperfections in the major roles. Step back from your critical feelings and view these players in a supportive light. Look at yourself and your idiosyncracy as an unconditionally loving, doting grandmother might. Can you, with this understanding viewpoint, smile fondly and embrace yourself, imperfection and all? If not, try using another version of Cecil's motto: "I make mistakes, but I like and accept myself, anyway!"

I love and accept myself even though I am imperfect.

I accept myself unconditionally.

Integrating Anger

INTEGRATING ANGER INTO OUR LIVES IS CRUCIALLY IMPORTANT TO our sense of well-being. Since much of women's depression is actually suppressed anger, allowing ourselves to feel and healthily accept our anger helps keep us out of the doldrums of debilitating depression.

Marie was sixty-one before she was able to understand why she felt increasingly depressed and dependent on her husband and daughters. After reading several self-help books, she joined a support group. Listening to a group member read a poem about his painful childhood opened a door for Marie. Through this portal poured years of buried anger, fear, and anxiety based on a painful family history, beginning with her separation from her family at age two.

The older the feelings, the younger the inner child experiencing them. Because those internal little ones need safe arms to hold them as they move through pain toward healing, Marie was very wise to find a group to support her. As Marie went through the dark woods of her childhood into the light of her present life, she needed torch-bearers for the journey—as do we all.

Along with her group support Marie found, through the following exercise, an inner friend who also encouraged her. Using her dominant right hand, Marie wrote questions such as: Marie, you are ten years old, how do you feel? With her left hand she answered: I feel like crying. As her experiment progressed, Marie's right-hand messages became those of a compassionate mother figure and her left hand took on the role of her inner child, the bearer of unhealed feelings.

As we begin to integrate our anger, we need to remember that feeling angry is only a part of the process toward a heartfelt awareness that what caused the anger was then, and we are fully capable of changing and healing our lives now.

I allow myself to be angry.

I move through anger into understanding and forgiveness.

I deserve to be supported as I move through difficult feelings.

Resting in Resistance

SO MANY OF US BELIEVE THAT WE NEED TO RESIST OUR RESISTANCE, not let it "get the best of us." But resistance may be a message from our wise inner self to stop, listen, and pay attention.

When she moved to New York from California, Lindsey fully intended to continue her nursing career, but she found herself resisting it at every turn. For a while she caused herself a lot of emotional pain by berating herself for being too fearful or lazy to find a nursing position. Finally, wisely, she decided to pay careful attention to her resistance. She attempted to decipher her dreams, she began meditating on her inner protest against nursing, and she wrote her reflections in a journal. As she slowly started trusting her resistance, Lindsey began to understand how burned out she was on nursing and that she needed to take a sabbatical.

Author Stephen Levine talks about the *fist of resistance* with which we block out our pain—emotional or physical—and, thereby, create suffering. Resistance can magnify any pain into suffering. Conversely, allowing ourselves to truly feel our woundedness and then gently surrounding it with love and mercy helps diminish pain.

With your eyes closed, allow yourself to deepen your breathing. Sink into the rhythm of your breath moving in and out of your body. Invite yourself to relax. Very gently give yourself permission to explore a resistance you are experiencing now. Watch your reaction as you think of this resistance. Move your attention to your heart and shine a soft, warm light on it. Feel the suppleness of your heart and encourage it to soften even more. Now, with no pressure or *have to's*, encourage your heart to open to the resistance and allow mercy, love, and acceptance to flow toward it.

We can learn to rest in our resistance, lean into it gently, and send it love and mercy rather than battling or suppressing it. As we sensitively trust and explore our resistance, we'll be able to uncover the undoubtedly wise *reason* for it.

I explore my resistance and, consequently, learn from it.

I know what is good for me.

Remembering to Breathe

ONE OF THE BEST WAYS TO FREE OUR FEELINGS IS TO BREATHE INTO them. Deep breathing assists us in several crucial ways. Physically, it cleanses our body of air that has been sapped of life-giving oxygen, replacing it with fresh, rejuvenating air. Interestingly, studies show that when elderly people practice deep breathing for only a few minutes a day, their memories improve dramatically.

Psychologically, slow, deliberate, deep breathing allows us to move below surface feelings into an awareness of causal, root emotions that may be breeding discomfort in our lives. Spiritually, deep breathing connects us to the flow of God's universe and anchors us firmly in our center, bringing us a sense of calm.

Yet, especially when we're tense or in crisis, we literally forget to breathe. This puts us in the position of attempting to cope while being deprived of vital oxygen. Very difficult to do.

Do yourself a life-enhancing favor. Remember to breathe deeply. Write a little note that says simply, *Breathe*, and refer to it several times a day, especially when you need to be sharp and at your best.

For years I was an amateur actress, and for many of those years I suffered from acute stage fright. To overcome the fear I learned a simple yoga exercise to do before going on stage. It included *breathing* and saying, "I'm glad you're here, I'm glad I'm here, and I know that I know!" I now do that same exercise when I speak in public. It makes a world of difference.

Practice breathing deeply for a few minutes right now. Arrange your body in a comfortable position and gently allow your breath to deepen, breathing in through your nose and out through your mouth. Imagine your body hungrily receiving these sustaining breaths and gratefully releasing its stale air. Thank your breath for its unfailing service to you.

The beautiful thing about remembering to breathe deeply is that we can do it anywhere, in any situation. It is guaranteed to improve things!

I am thankful for my breath.

In times of crisis I remember to breathe deeply.

Answering "Present!"

FEELING BORED OR OVERWHELMED MAY MEAN THAT WE ARE approaching life like an apathetic teenager going to school—not present with enthusiasm but rather attending in a fog of indifference. If we play hooky from life by automatically doing what has to be done but savoring nothing, we're robbing ourselves of the chance to vigorously *feel* and *live* life. We are not answering "Present!" when Life calls the roll.

In order to feel vitally alive and live up to our creative potential, we need to make a commitment to being present in our lives, up front and paying attention, not just slumped in the back row apathetically waiting for the bell to ring.

Brittany was considering dropping out of college because she felt it was boring, useless, and too much work. Underneath those feelings was a sense of failure and futility over her low grades. A fellow student shared with Brittany a tip she had gotten from a study video called "Where There's a Will, There's an A": *Sit in the front row in all classes.* Not totally trusting such a simple solution but wanting to succeed, Brittany decided to try.

She was uncomfortable at first, but soon she began to look forward to getting to classes early in order to ensure herself a seat up front. Instructors who had seemed aloof and dull now often talked directly to her and recognized her on campus. Her enthusiasm for her courses took an astounding forward leap and, at the end of the semester, her grades reflected her interest.

Encouraging ourselves to sit in the front row of life invites us to be attentive to and appreciative of all its varied aspects. When we answer, "Present!" we'll be rewarded by *conscious* living in which we are aware of our feelings, rather than separated from them.

I give myself the gift of sitting up front in my life.
I pay attention.
I have a right to really experience my feelings.

Mining the Gold of Dreams

OUR DREAMS ARE A GOLD MINE OF INFORMATION. NOT ONLY DO they siphon off excess energy and anxiety, but they can also inspire and educate us. Dreams give us a glimpse into both our subconscious and unconscious minds and allow us to access parts of ourselves often veiled in the glare of daily existence. Dreams are movies in which we are the sole director, actor, producer, and creator; yet, how often do we intentionally attend these movies and allow ourselves to be entertained and enlightened?

Julia, a client of mine, was vaguely discontent but couldn't understand why. We explored one of her dreams in which she was hospitalized and unwillingly subjected to many procedures. In the dream she felt powerless to voice her opinion. Everyone else seemed to know what was good for her and would not listen to any of her suggestions.

Exploring this dream gave Julia nugget after nugget of insight about her lifelong habit of allowing others to make her choices for her. By recognizing her tendency to unquestioningly comply with others, she saw that a large part of her unhappiness stemmed from feeling powerless in her marriage. Using her dream as an indicator of her feelings, Julia worked on expressing herself and stating her preferences. Slowly she gained the confidence to make her own decisions and speak up for herself. In the process of owning her power, her listlessness diminished and she began feeling happier.

A good way to tap into the wisdom of your dreams is to keep a pen and paper by your bed. Immediately after you wake up, replay the dream and then jot down some shorthand notes that will help you reclaim the dream. Later, you can go back and fill in the details.

Spend time with your dreams. Rerun them. Symbolically take the pickax of your intuition into the gold mine of your dreams, knowing that their meaning will be revealed to you as you take the time to mine the treasure.

I easily remember my dreams.

I enjoy studying my dreams and readily interpret them.

Ringing True

ANNE FRANK, WHO WAS WISE BEYOND HER YEARS, SAID, "EVERYONE has inside him a piece of the good news. The good news is that you don't know how great you can be! How much you can love! What you can accomplish! And what your potential is!" In her brief time, Anne nourished and expressed her authentic self through introspection and writing and, consequently, has posthumously touched and inspired countless hearts.

One of our most important tasks is to recognize in ourselves what Anne Frank terms "the good news." How great can we be? How much love are we capable of giving? What accomplishments wait to be achieved? What vast potential beckons? Only through feeding our authenticity will we be able to fully dramatize our good news, our potential, our gifts to the world.

Feeding our authenticity consists of many things, including being aware of and honoring our true feelings, accepting ourselves totally, listening to our inner voice, supporting and encouraging ourselves, comforting and nurturing ourselves, giving ourselves permission to act independently, accepting help when we need it, and making space for solitude and creativity.

Being true to ourselves is the most important way we can feed our authenticity. Take a few minutes now to quietly tune into yourself. Gently feel yourself sinking into the center of your being. Block out distractions to the best of your ability, and give yourself your undivided attention. Allow your breathing to deepen. Inhale slowly through your nose and exhale slowly through your mouth.

Bring into your mind's eye an image of yourself as a beautiful bell in a steeple. If the bell you first sense doesn't please you, change it until both its sight and sound are uplifting to you. Listen with love, acceptance, and admiration as your bell melodiously peals out the good news of your authenticity.

If our steeple bell—the unique and authentic self at the center of our being—is to chime and charm the entire valley of which we are a part, then it must ring true!

I accept the good news that I am great.

I am true to myself.

Becoming an Inner Environmentalist

WE ARE BECOMING MORE RESPONSIBLE FOR OUR PLANET BY adopting environmentally conscious ways of living on Mother Earth in the fervent hope that she will thrive and continue to support us. But equally important to our lives is an increased awareness of the detrimental consequences of inner pollution, caused by self-condemnation, unsupportive relationships, exhausting schedules, unhealed emotional wounds, and a lack of spiritual conviction.

If we are to feel comforted rather than criticized and encouraged rather than futile, we must become an inner environmentalist, cleaning out unwanted feelings and clearing a space for health and wholeness. If your inner pain is deep-seated and of long standing, resulting from such traumatic experiences as incest or child abuse, please do not try to handle it alone. Find a therapist or friend who can compassionately and tolerantly stand by you as you courageously sort, discard, and heal unwanted feelings that are polluting your life.

As a small step toward cleaning and clearing, visualize your inner environment as a garage. Is it cluttered with the debris of old pain, impossible expectations, and devaluing assumptions? Is it polluted by the stench of resentment, envy, or self-condemnation? If so, begin to take out the trash! In your mind's eye, dispose of unwanted and outdated emotional rubbish in ways that feel the most freeing to you, even to the point of tearing down and rebuilding the entire garage if that seems to be the right thing to do. When you've finished, survey the newly cleaned or reconstructed garage and savor the order you have restored to it.

No matter where our emotional garbage originated, it is our responsibility now to discard it, heal it, and free ourselves from it. It is possible, with commitment and courage, to become happy, healthy, and emotionally uncluttered.

*I have the courage to face and cleanse
my inner pollution.*

I ask for encouragement and support when I need it.

Removing the Cauldron from the Fire

FROM TIME TO TIME, WE FIND OURSELVES EMBROILED IN A CAULDRON of discontent, stewing over things we wish were different. When this happens, we can choose to remove the cauldron from the fire by changing our focus to action rather than reaction. For when we allow our cauldron of negative feelings to remain too long in the fire, we become hard-boiled.

One day, when all four of my kids were still at home, I was preparing dinner in a fit of resentment. Good grief!—one of them could almost always be counted on to turn up a nose at the meal I'd cooked. I stomped around the kitchen wondering why I had to prepare all the meals. I added more worms and spiders' eyes to my bitch's brew by chastising myself for not having the guts to *demand* more help. My victimized self-talk had just gotten my internal cauldron almost to the boiling point when I glanced at a little saying stenciled on my recipe box: Lord, help me add a dash of love!

That saying stopped me in my tracks. It certainly wasn't love—either for myself or for my family—that I'd been adding to the dinner. What could I do to remove my cauldron from the fire and be able to honestly add a dash of love when I cooked? For me, the most important realization was how angry I felt over being the only cook. With that understanding, I was able to change my focus from resentment to possible solutions, including initiating a cook's night off at least once a week.

Gently center yourself in whatever way works for you, and allow to float into your mind a situation that causes your internal cauldron to boil. What angers you or causes you resentment? Have you allowed yourself to feel victimized by the circumstances? What dash of love *toward yourself* do you need to add to the equation in order to start changing the situation? Gently assure your-self that you have the right and responsibility to transform these feelings, and commit to supporting yourself in removing your caul-dron from the fire.

I have the courage to be assertive.

*I listen to my feelings and act on them
when appropriate.*

Letting the Shadow Roam

According to Carl Jung, the shadow parts of ourselves are undeveloped or denied aspects of our beings that need to be acknowledged. If we were brought up to be "nice" girls, for example, we were probably also taught to be ashamed of our shadow—our rage, assertiveness, ambition, sexuality, even our creativeness—denying and repressing it to the detriment of our well-being.

Denied, our shadow gains strength and becomes almost diabolical in its ability to cause us, and others, pain. But when we embrace our shadowy aspects and learn to express them in *constructive* ways, their energy is transformed and, therefore, able to merge in a healthy way with our other parts.

When Allie discovered that her husband was having an affair, her immediate desire was to kill both him and the woman. Terrified by her reaction, she quickly quelled that very natural shadow response and instead began feeling that it was her fault he had strayed. She became increasingly depressed until she could hardly move from the couch. She eventually dragged herself to see me.

It required a lot of encouragement from me for Allie to face her shadow. Beneath her depression she was boiling with rage, the power of which absolutely petrified her. When she was finally satisfied that it was okay to have such emotions, but that they needed to be acted on *constructively*, she began letting her shadow roam. She threw eggs at trees and wrote volumes of hate letters to her betrayers and then burned them.

Most important, Allie stopped judging herself for her emotions and began to really feel empowered by her shadow. In the process, she realized that her biggest contribution to the cracking of her marriage had been her inability to be her own person. Although it has been a long and difficult road, happily, Allie and her husband are in the process of creating a new, healthier marriage.

Like the dark side of the moon, our shadow is ever present. It is up to us to liberate and illuminate it.

I am a nice person even though I have ugly feelings.

I invite my shadow out to play.

Melting Stress through Motion

LAKES OR PONDS FED BY MOVING WATER REMAIN FRESH AND CLEAR. Similarly, by encouraging ourselves to *move*, we can transform unwanted emotional stagnation into vitality. Putting ourselves *in motion* can help us achieve the e-motions we would like to have.

Physically, movement facilitates circulation and helps the body process the nutrients it needs; mentally, putting the body into action helps us clear out the cobwebs and makes us sharper. Feeling better physically and keener mentally, in and of itself, makes our emotions more harmonious. We just plain feel better about ourselves when we move.

Different types of motion serve different purposes. Yoga and Tai Chi are meditative practices that are excellent physical disciplines as well as being useful for centering, calming, and comforting ourselves. Martial arts help us hone our bodies and our minds. Walking, biking, and aerobic dance are wonderful for reducing stress and tension.

Carla, a special-education teacher, tries never to miss her three-times-a-week aerobic class. She uses it for both physical and emotional fitness. If she has had a sad or frustrating experience with one of her students, a parent, or the administration, she puts her objects of anger in front of her and pretends to punch them each time she moves. As she visualizes the culprits reeling from her cuffing, she can feel her stress and tension melting away.

Encourage yourself to get up and move right now. We still have within us that spontaneous child who intuitively knows how to *dance toward balance and harmony*. Invite her out to play. Let her remind you of the transformative value of unrehearsed motion.

I enjoy being in motion.

I choose the form of exercise and movement
that is right for me and commit to doing it.

I allow my inner child to dance and
play spontaneously.

Paying Attention
to Our Body Wisdom

To keep a lamp burning we have to
keep putting oil in it.

—Mother Teresa

OUR PHYSICAL BODIES ARE INTERWOVEN WITH OUR emotional, mental, and spiritual bodies. Each needs to be maintained, healed, and honored for the whole to work optimally. Having the courage to accept, be grateful for, and love our bodies, no matter how they look or feel is difficult for many of us. But it is important that we befriend our bodies because they are the vessels containing our essence, the vehicles through which we express life. Without the cooperation of our bodies, we as we know ourselves would not exist. If someone gave us a magnificent, expensive car that functioned smoothly and got us where we needed to go in absolute comfort, we would take care of it—keep it clean, give it gas, oil, and tuneups. We have been given such a gift in the form of our bodies, which are incredible machines, more wondrous than we can imagine. They deserve our respect, care, and appreciation.

Stimulating Our Natural Healing

WE USED TO BELIEVE THAT ILLNESS WAS SOMETHING OVER WHICH we had absolutely no control. If we were sick or injured there was no choice but to put our fate in the hands of doctors. With research, medical experts now know that a patient is much more in control of her healing than was previously believed. Our attitudes, beliefs, and emotions all affect how we heal. Challenging the old beliefs that we need to turn complete responsibility for our health over to someone else is a courageous decision to make.

We are exposed to germs daily, yet some of us seem more susceptible to illness than others. Why? Perhaps those who get sick expect illness as a part of life or feel victimized by germs. If so, the message we are giving our bodies is that we fear they are weak and defenseless. When this is what we believe, our immune system will be less effective and our bodies more prone to disease.

Our physical bodies need encouragement and reassurance just as our emotional, mental, and spiritual bodies do. Whenever we feel a cold coming on or seem especially vulnerable to disease, we can have the courage to feel empowered rather than victimized by immediately thanking our body for its incredible immune system. We can picture our resourceful white blood cells easing out any unwanted bacteria and visualize ourselves feeling well and energized. Over the next few hours we should continue to thank our bodies for their wonderful functioning. Of course, it's also prudent to pop vitamin C.

While not a substitute for necessary medical care, affirming health and the perfect working of our immune system is a powerful tool we can use to stimulate our natural healing abilities.

*My immune system is perfectly balanced
and able to heal my body.*

My body is strong and resilient.

Encouraging Our Body

NOT PAYING MUCH ATTENTION TO WHAT I WAS DOING ONE DAY while making muffins, I stuck the spatula into the running blades of the mixer. Quickly the spatula was sucked into the blades as were three of my fingers. The poor mixer kept grinding away as I stared in shock at my vibrating hand. After what seemed like minutes, but was probably nanoseconds, I jerked the cord out of the socket. Now the problem was how to get my hand out. I was alone so it was me versus the mixer.

When I did manage to pull my fingers free, they were the color of skim milk and each had a large, deep dent in it. Feeling faint and nauseated I slumped at the table saying, "Oh, no." But deep inside my head I felt the message, "You can heal this now." So, as I soaked my hand in ice water, I began to thank my body for its amazing healing powers and pictured my hand as it had been minutes before—pain-free and fully functional. I talked to my hand as a nurturing mother would talk to an injured child, assuring it everything would be okay. I even kissed it, as one would a child, to make it "all better." Amazingly, within two hours you could not even see the dents and the only discomfort I had was a slight stiffness in one finger.

Our bodies listen to us. We can help our minds heal our bodies by the way we choose to speak. And it doesn't have to be an emergency to use this technique. By lovingly talking to your body each day, you can help it stay strong and healthy.

My body is a miraculous healing machine.
I love and trust my body.
I gently encourage my body when it is in need of healing.

Paying Attention to Our Body Wisdom

OFTEN WE PAY TOO LITTLE ATTENTION TO THE SIGNALS OUR BODIES send us. But when we ignore the signals, our bodies may grab our attention in creative ways. Chris was going through an extremely stressful divorce and felt depleted by emotional and financial strain. Through exhaustion and an outbreak of acne, her body told her to take time to rest and replenish her energies. She ignored its messages and buried herself in work and other commitments, pushing herself to the point of collapse.

Then a small cyst developed in her ear lobe. She ignored that, too. So her body had little choice but to send a more graphic message. The cyst became enlarged until her ear was a painful and grotesque three times its normal size. With an ear that big, and being called "Dumbo" by her coworkers, how could she continue to not hear what her body was telling her? Doctors said the cause of the cyst was stress. She got the message. As she began to slow down, her ear began to go down.

Since we often fear appearing lazy, it is especially courageous for us to follow the advice of our bodies when they tell us to rest and relax. However, we can choose to listen to and honor our bodies' messages. Paying attention to our bodies allows their instinctive wisdom to help us stay healthy.

I pay close attention to my body.
I respect my body and honor its needs.
I am alert to the signals my body sends me.

Balancing and Harmonizing Ourselves

MUCH OF OUR PAIN, BOTH PHYSICAL AND EMOTIONAL, STEMS FROM a lack of harmony in all aspects of our being. When we are sick, our immune systems are busily working to bring our bodies back into balance. When we are upset, our emotions are yearning for a sense of rightness and harmony.

We greatly assist ourselves in staying finely tuned when we honor the four aspects of our being—physical, emotional, mental, and spiritual—and give each of them daily, positive attention. If paying attention to our own needs feels self-indulgent, it will take a lot of courage for us to persevere in caring for all four aspects each day. But we can.

Some examples of positive attention to our physical selves are exercising, eating well, and sleeping enough; to our emotional selves are sharing with a friend, writing in a journal, having a good cry, and helping someone else; to our mental selves are learning a new game, catching that creative thought, and cooking a challenging meal; and to our spiritual selves are praying/meditating, appreciating nature, reading uplifting materials, and spending quality time with our kids.

Having the courage and discipline to balance our lives leads to a more healthy, harmonious, and joyful existence.

Each day I give the physical, emotional, mental,
and spiritual aspects of my being loving attention.

I have the courage and discipline to live a balanced life.

I enjoy staying finely tuned.

Appreciating Our Bodies

WOMEN OFTEN HATE THEIR BODIES. WE HAVE LEARNED BODY SHAME from comparing ourselves with the flawless beauties we see in magazines and movies. We fail to appreciate our own inner and outer beauty if they don't live up to the ideal given us, in large part, by the advertising industry.

One way for us to escape the tyranny of unattainable ad agency ideals is to change our focus from criticism to appreciation. We can begin by concentrating on how faithfully our bodies work for us, and praise them for functioning well. Our bodies deserve and desire our appreciation. We have nothing to be ashamed of, no matter how we look.

Doing the following exercise takes a great deal of courage if we have been taught to be embarrassed or ashamed of our bodies. If the exercise is difficult, it's very important that we gently take one small step at a time. Stand in front of the mirror (nude is good, but if that feels too uncomfortable, don't do it) and survey your body. Notice the places toward which you feel particularly critical. Even if you don't feel this way right now, tell these places that you love and appreciate them. Think of specific things about these parts of your body you are thankful for. Say these out loud, "Legs, I am thankful you are strong enough for me to walk on the beach." Now do the same for your body as a whole, such as "Body, thank you for allowing me to hold little babies and pet cats."

In order to accept and appreciate ourselves as we are, we need to have the courage to give up our negative feelings toward our bodies.

I love and appreciate my body.

I am proud of my body and what it can do.

I am thankful for my body,
which is my vehicle for moving through life.

Being the Right Weight

ONE OF THE BIGGEST TORMENTS OF MANY WOMEN'S EXISTENCE IS the pain of weight gain. Our self-esteem can plummet as our weight inches upward and we inch outward. In addition, we know we are healthier, have more energy, and feel better about ourselves when we are at our correct and healthy weight. Why, then, do we ride the roller coaster of lose-gain over and over again? Why do our good intentions about eating properly and losing forever those extra pounds often end in failure?

It is difficult to maintain our best weight partly because doing so feels like deprivation. We reward ourselves with comforting foods such as chocolate and starch, and when those comforts are removed we often feel depressed.

Perhaps one of the secrets to happily being our optimum weight is to change the pleasure/pain link-up in our minds. Do we link losing and maintaining a healthy weight with the pain of deprivation or the pleasure of being able to admire our reflection in the mirror? Do we concentrate on the pain of giving up some foods or the pleasure of gaining more energy and being able to wear different clothes? Focusing on the pleasure of attaining our goal, and not on the pain of getting and staying there, gives us a much better chance of having the bodies we long for.

Allow yourself to sit quietly, eyes closed, and bring into your mind's eye a realistic and attractive picture of the way you would like to look. Visualize yourself at the perfect weight for your build, age, and lifestyle. Enjoy the picture of yourself at this weight, begin to imagine all the benefits you will have from being this size. Soak in the pleasure that reaching your goal will bring you, and gently encourage yourself toward it.

*I concentrate on the pleasure
of being my right weight.*

*I appreciate my body
and take good care of it.*

Aging as an Attitude

THERE ARE THINGS WE CAN DO TO KEEP FROM FEELING OLD. Exercise, eat well, have love in our lives, be of service. But probably the most important way to feel young is to remember that *age is an attitude*. What we think about aging determines how we feel about it.

Elaine, one of the youngest people I know, is seventy-nine years old. What makes her young? She is enthusiastic about almost everything, is still working at her profession, is sincerely interested in other people and, since she continues to be open-minded about new ideas, is learning fresh things all the time. Best of all she is fun to be around.

You might think she has such a great attitude because her life has been easy. No. Her first child died in infancy; three of her five other children had polio at the same time and one was left crippled; money has always been tight; and she, too, has physical challenges. But her attitude is "Aren't I lucky! Isn't it fun to be alive."

When we have the courage to move through any fears we may have about aging and find answers to the questions that bother us, whether they are of a spiritual or physical nature, we can then have the peace of mind to age with an attitude of gratitude and expectancy.

I love and accept the age I am now.

I feel vital, enthusiastic, and energetic.

*I have the courage to face my fears about aging
and share them with people I trust.*

Highlighting the Positives of Aging

THERE ARE CULTURES THAT REVERE AGE, IN WHICH RESPECT FOR A person increases as the years progress, and older is actually seen as wiser. Ours is not one of them. We still generally subscribe to the youth-is-better conviction. Individually, we have the power to choose a philosophy where older, in fact, can be better.

Energy flows where attention goes and we are in charge of what we pay attention to. If we choose to focus on the negatives about aging, our energy will flow in that direction and become depleted. However, when we courageously choose to concentrate on the positives of aging, our energy will be expanded.

After I turned forty-five or so, I could have chosen to focus on the fact that "hot-flash" was a term I was well acquainted with, or that when I looked in the mirror my mother's face often looked back at me. Instead I decided to concentrate on the positive aspects of aging (or "saging" as some call it), such as having the freedom to pursue my own interests and feeling sure of myself, more often than not.

We can all choose where we focus our attention, and that will determine how we feel as the birthdays roll by. Sit quietly, close your eyes and bring into the theater of your mind a picture or sense of yourself five years from now. See yourself happy, healthy, and enjoying life. Give yourself the qualities you would like to possess, or expand the positive qualities you already have. Absorb what it feels like to enjoy those qualities. Appreciate yourself at this age. Now see yourself aging in five-year increments, and love and appreciate yourself at each of those ages. Enjoy the wonderful old woman you will become.

I highlight the positives of being

_____ years old.

I enjoy and celebrate myself.

I love who I am and who I am becoming.

Oiling Our Apparatus Aerobically

OFTEN OUR LIVES ARE SO HECTIC WE FEEL WE MUST CUT CORNERS somewhere in order to have time for everything. Exercise is frequently one of the things we cut. Yet, if we do not exercise aerobically at least three times a week, we are wreaking havoc on our bodies. Aerobic exercise is necessary to oxygenate our blood, revitalize our immune system, and keep our muscles healthy and supple.

Aerobic exercise is also good for the psyche. When we are depressed, sad, or confused, exercising helps us dispel the cobwebs. That's because one of the greatest side benefits of aerobic exercise is the reduction of stress. We can begin exercising feeling stressed and depressed, and end the session feeling relaxed and alert through the body's release of its natural tranquilizers.

When our bodies are fit, well-oiled with exercise, everything else becomes easier. Starting small is important so that we do not get discouraged—we can take a ten-minute walk, or ride a bike for five minutes—and, if possible, it's good to make a pact with a friend in order to support and encourage each other. The hardest part of exercising consistently is initially making the decision, and then setting aside the time in our schedule. Chances are, if we can stick to an exercise program for six months, we'll be so happy with how we feel, that we'll be hooked—and healthier—for life. Although it can be difficult, being kind to ourselves by having the courage to commit to an aerobic exercise program will enhance our health and sense of well-being.

I enjoy exercising.
I make time to give my body the
exercise it wants and needs.

Recognizing Rainbows

The miracles of the church seem to me
to rest not so much upon faces or voices or
healing power coming suddenly near to us from afar, but
upon our perceptions being made finer,
so that for a moment our eyes can see and
our ears can hear what is there
about us always.

—Willa Cather

WHEN WE ARE AT OUR BEST—LISTENING TO AND HONORING our inner natures—we can tune in to frequencies within ourselves and others that are filled with the beauty, hope, and inspiration of rainbows. Don't we, when catching sight of a rainbow, automatically breathe an awed, "Oh!"? Rainbows are awe inspiring, partially because they are fleeting and magical. Even though they can be explained scientifically, they affect our hearts, not our minds.

We can all have the courage to look beyond the mundane to the miraculous, to recognize our own unique rainbows. Because I have worked for years with people who are dying and bereaved, and been blessed by their sharings, some of the stories I use will give you a peek through the veil we call death.

Recognizing Rainbows

IT IS EASY FOR US TO ARMOR OUR HEARTS AGAINST PAIN SO DILIGENTLY that we also close them to the appreciation of precious everyday miracles. I like to think of rainbows as God's equivalent to Hallmark greeting cards, a way of saying, "Hi there. I love you, and I'm around whether you can see me or not." Rainbows, notes from The Divine made up of light and color, are everywhere if we have the eyes and the heart to see them—a child's open smile, an unexpected call from a friend, a creative new idea, or the sight of an elderly couple holding hands.

Bonnie was driving down the freeway in Hawaii and noticed the cars in front of her swerving slightly to avoid something in the road. Thrusting its head bravely through a crack in the pavement was a flower! With misty eyes she told me she saw that courageous little flower as a rainbow, telling her it was possible for us all to bloom even in the hardest situations and most people can be trusted not to run over us if they can help it. It was a message she badly needed to hear right then.

In order to relish the rainbows of life, we need the ability to laugh and be happy. Freeing our spontaneous and wonder-filled inner child from the confines of "adulthood" will allow us to play more at life rather than working so hard at it. It is through the innocent eyes of our healed inner child, and in an atmosphere of spontaneous joy, that we can recognize the rainbows our hearts have known forever.

Having the courage to open our hearts to miracles allows us to enjoy and learn from our rainbow messengers.

*Each day I open my heart
to recognize the rainbows in my life.*

I bloom even in difficult situations.

God is loving me now.

Opening to Miracles

FREQUENTLY WE ARE SO "DULLED BY DOING" WE LOSE OUR CHILDLIKE eyes and are blinded to the rainbows of grace that come our way.

A short time after my mother's death, I was sitting in my kitchen talking to a friend about Mother's last few days. A moment after I told her that Mother had wished she could "fly away like a little bird and never come back," a tiny hummingbird came to the window where it hovered, looking directly at me, for several seconds. The hairs stood up on my arms and tears came to my eyes. I felt as if the little bird were giving me a message from Mother—reassuring me that "Even though you can't see me, I am with you." The adult in me could chalk it all up to coincidence, but my miracle-loving child firmly believes it was a heavenly love note.

We need to have the courage to go against the current of society which demands we do so much that we forget to be, and take time to open our eyes and hearts to the miracles that surround us daily. We can look at our world through the awestruck eyes of our inner child and be deeply enriched by doing so.

Today, as you go about your usual routine, try a little experiment. Look at your surroundings and at the people you encounter with the unabashed curiosity of a child. For a least a few seconds, see your world through eyes that expect a miracle.

I take time to open my eyes and heart to miracles.

I allow my inner child to revel in everyday blessings.

I have the courage to believe in the miraculous.

Focusing on Beauty

WHEN WE ARE IN PAIN OR CONFUSION AND OUR MINDS STUBBORNLY gnaw on the source, it is often healing to refocus our thoughts on beauty. Remembering to change our focus and finding the self-discipline to do so is courageous.

Janet was going through a painful divorce. Once, when her heart was ragged and bleeding, she sat behind her soon-to-be-ex-husband at their son's Little League game. Her husband and his girlfriend were snuggling and giggling throughout the game. Janet longed to leave but did not want to disappoint her son. Nervously picking at the grass, she noticed she was sitting by a clump of wildflowers that had tiny blue blooms. To ease her heart, she began to focus on the flowers. They were beautiful and delicate, each a little different from its sister, perfect. . . .

To Janet's surprise she began to feel peace seeping into every crevice of her being, and she felt completely loved. She realized if God cared enough to create the astounding beauty of those little weeds in the middle of a school yard, God must also love her, even in the middle of her emotional wasteland.

Mother Nature is healing. She surrounds us with beauty that can bind our wounds and delight our hearts if we let it. We need to relate to her—get dirt under our nails. Even if we live in an apartment in the middle of Manhattan, we can have flowers that lift their little faces to us in gratitude for the water and food we give them. The miraculous beauty of even the simplest flower can give our hearts a boost if we have the courage and willingness to take the time to really see and savor it.

Give yourself the gift of looking into the face of a flower. Take time with it. Appreciate the miracle of it.

I fill myself with the beauty and peace of nature.

*I have the courage to focus on beauty
even in the midst of pain.*

Reaching through the Veil

DIANE'S DAUGHTER, SALLY, DIED OF BONE CANCER WHEN SHE WAS thirty-one. During the last few days of her life she was comatose off and on, so weak she could barely move. But one day she sat upright, looked toward the foot of her bed and exclaimed, "Grandma, you're so young!" Later, when Sally regained consciousness, Diane asked her if she had seen her grandmother. She answered peacefully, "Oh, yes, Grandma is waiting for me!" Grandma had died when Sally was three years old.

Stories such as these can help alleviate our fear of death and dying. In the very depths of our hearts we can come to believe we never die alone—that there are always loved ones and escorts to greet us. This belief can also help us realize we do not live alone either; there are always people willing and able to be with us and help us when we need it.

Solace and understanding are available to us when we have the courage to reach through the veil of our resistance or shame and ask for what we want and need. Opening our hearts to the awareness that we are always loved and never alone brings us the security and peace of mind for which we all yearn. The veil between us and the divine is more permeable than we imagine.

I trust I am never alone.

I am loved and protected in this life and beyond.

*I have the courage to open myself
to the love that surrounds me.*

Seeing with the Eyes of Innocence

WHEN MY SONS WERE LITTLE I ALWAYS TUCKED THEM INTO BED WITH a prayer asking their guardian angels to watch over them as they slept. As I began to learn about phenomena such as ESP, near-death experiences, and the wonders of mystics and shamans, it occurred to me to find out if they ever saw their guardian angels. When I asked, they looked at me with their innocent four- and six-year-old eyes and said, "Sure! Don't you?" Unfortunately, no. I had lost my innocence and openness to the miraculous as I moved into the serious reality of adulthood. But my little boys helped me recapture a sense of wonder and awe.

Courageously allowing ourselves to become aware of our world through the eyes of innocence—to grow young—opens up a vista of external and internal beauty easily missed if our nose is always pressed to the grown-up grindstone. We can practice looking at things with the eyes of an enthusiastic four-year-old and experience similar wonder.

Sit quietly, with your eyes closed, and open your inner, inno-cent eyes. Invite into your presence one or more compassionate and beautiful angels. As you visualize these exquisite Beings of Light, open yourself to absorb the love, strength, and peace of mind that emanates from them. Invite them to re-parent you by loving you exactly as you are now. Allow yourself to become a cherished and valued child of these Beings.

I am valuable and lovable.
I allow myself to absorb
love and acceptance from others.
I have the courage to know I am worthy.

Emulating Butterflies

BECAUSE BUTTERFLIES ARE DEEPLY SYMBOLIC OF OUR OWN STRUGGLE to grow into our unique beauty and wisdom, they bring a smile to our faces. As with the swan, which also grows into its beauty and grace, the butterfly in its immature larva stage is not at all appealing. But, following a deep inner knowing, it goes into seclusion to allow its destiny to unfold. Protecting itself from outside distractions, it retreats to the darkness and isolation of its cocoon. In due time, as promised by its inner wisdom, it emerges as a winged creature and spends the rest of its life spreading beauty and joy as it gently flies from flower to flower—a symbol of hope and transformation.

As we move through the chaos, confusion, and challenges of everyday life, we should remember we have a winged and wonderful Self within us, waiting to emerge from the darkness. Like the butterfly, we need only go into the stillness and solitude—to look within—to find our wise Inner-Self waiting to transform us through her knowing embrace.

Being gentle and patient with ourselves as we go within is essential. Transformation takes time, commitment, and discipline. Each day we need to give ourselves the blessing of a few quiet minutes of cocooning. We can have the courage to trust the cocooning process and not expect spectacular fireworks or even insights at first. It takes a while for our minds to become quiet enough for us to hear the flutter of our inner wings.

I trust my inner butterfly.

*I take a few quiet minutes each day
to tune into my inner self.*

*Each day I am more able to hear
the quiet whispers of my inner wings.*

Laughing with Our Klutz

IT TAKES COURAGE TO LAUGH, TO HAVE A SENSE OF HUMOR. WHY? Because when something is really funny it is a reflection of our own foibles and weaknesses, those things about ourselves which make us cringe. To have a good sense of humor, we must be able to not take ourselves too seriously—to increase our ability to laugh with, not at, ourselves as we stumble and stagger through the comedy of life.

This is especially difficult for women because we have been taught that how we look is incredibly important. As girls we were definitely encouraged to be aware of what the neighbors would think, and that left many of us fearful of being judged if we acted in an unladylike manner. Becoming comfortable with ourselves when we have egg on our faces as well as when we are doing things perfectly is a challenge, but ultimately makes us more fun to be around.

Barbara was terrified of appearing foolish in front of others because she was afraid they would reject her. But that was really only her surface belief. Her deep, underlying conviction was that she was only lovable if she was perfect. When she began to change that belief by assuring herself she would love herself as a queen or a klutz, in strength and vulnerability, slim or chubby, she began to enjoy herself more. In fact, she has become so good at loving and reassuring her insecure inner child that she actually gets a kick out of her klutzy self now.

We can do as Barbara did. Instead of seeing our klutzy self as a part of us we must hide, we can choose to view her as a charming and irresistible free spirit.

I have the courage to take myself lightly.

*I am a worthwhile and capable woman
even though I make mistakes.*

Putting a Little Play in Our Day

ONE OF OUR BIGGEST CHALLENGES CAN BE ALLOWING OURSELVES THE seeming luxury of playing during our busy days. Play isn't necessarily a time-consuming activity; play also can be an attitude.

Jeannie works as activities director at a retirement home. In an environment that could be sobering and serious, she has decided to inject an attitude of playfulness. Jeannie cultivates her ability to delight in and lighten up the mundane and serious business of day-to-day living. She taps into her spontaneous inner child by trying to look at each day as an event to be celebrated. She dresses in costume (simple and homemade) for all holidays and sometimes just because . . . But more importantly, she allows her ready and raucous laughter to bounce uninhibitedly down the corridors of her workplace and her life. Jeannie is her own best playmate, and her example is helping the residents of her facility adopt an attitude of playfulness in their lives.

Reminding ourselves to incorporate an attitude of playfulness into our day can be done by putting little cards around saying, for instance, IT'S OK TO PLAY, I PUT A LITTLE PLAY IN MY DAY, or LIFE—FOR THE FUN OF IT. Often keeping ourselves aware of our desired change is the only impetus we need to lighten up.

Sit quietly (maybe holding a teddy bear), close your eyes, and invite into your mind's theater a spontaneous child who is filled with wonder at all life—a child with whom you would like to be best friends. Create a place filled with marvelous things to play with and exciting spots to explore. Have fun. Enjoy each other and your time together.

Getting in the habit of inviting your new friend to be a part of your everyday life gives you a chance to learn from her how to enjoy, to be in childlike joy, daily.

I encourage myself to play and have fun.
I am my own best playmate.
I enjoy having an attitude of playfulness.

Detaching Compassionately through Play

MOST OF US HAVE OTHERS IN OUR LIVES, OFTEN FAMILY MEMBERS, whom we allow to emotionally sabotage us. After encountering them, we either seethe with frustration or are saturated with guilt. Learning to compassionately detach from such people is one of the most courageous and empowering things we can do for ourselves.

Sandy spent years feeling guilt-ridden and frustrated over her alcoholic brother. He was convinced she had received all the love and attention from their parents and that her success was the reason for his failure. No amount of rational communication, refuting, or compassion changed his mind. She was always the bad guy in his eyes. Having tried many unsuccessful ways of unhooking, Sandy decided she had nothing to lose by playing at it rather than working so hard.

During their next conversation her brother's poor-me, if-it-wasn't-for-you litany began but she handled it differently. She visualized cartoon hooks flying all around her, and she whisked them away with her hands saying (silently, since they were on the phone), "I won't have any hooks today, thank you!" Sandy began to really enjoy herself, batting away all the old and ugly hooks that used to pierce her.

When Sandy began taking her brother's comments less seriously, she was able to remain open to him. Eventually, without her resistance to keep him fueled and fired up, he began to act differently. We can unhook from trying to change another person's mind, save him or her, or defend ourselves, and we can do it playfully.

*I have the courage to compassionately detach
from others when necessary.*

I lighten up about things that irritate me.

Nestling in the Arms of Nature

THE DIFFICULT ADJUSTMENT OF MOVING FROM HAWAII TO California was eased for me when I learned how to nestle in the arms of trees. The Sisters, as I had named two straight and regal pine trees at the edge of my new backyard forest, beckoned me to visit. But I was bustling about doing the business of settling in. One day, however, when I felt especially lonely, housebound, and resentful, I remembered someone telling me about the benefits of hugging a tree.

Extricating myself from packing boxes and pictures needing to be hung, I made my way through the blackberries and undergrowth to the base of The Sisters. Collapsing between them, I began to relax. To my great surprise, I started to cry. In the presence of these two trees, friends from the moment I first laid eyes on them, I became aware of feelings I'd been suppressing. Through my tears I began to talk aloud. A sense of acceptance, comfort, and peace floated through me as I bared my soul to The Sisters. I was able to return to my chores renewed and refreshed.

Nature is pure, patient, and nonjudgmental; she accepts us all, and we all need her acceptance. The love of Mother Nature can help us all when we have the courage to open to it.

Sit quietly. With your eyes closed, create a beautiful place in nature, either real or imaginary, and begin to enjoy the sounds and sights around you. Familiarize yourself with the area and then settle comfortably into your favorite space. Accept and absorb the peace and comfort of this little oasis. Open to the strength that emanates from both the living and inanimate objects. Bask in this beauty and strength and allow it to become a healing and soothing part of you.

I take the time to be in and appreciate nature.

*I am comforted
by the strength and beauty of nature.*

Claiming the Goddess Within

What woman needs is not as a woman to act or rule, but as a nature to grow, as an intellect to discern, as a soul to live freely and unimpeded, to unfold such powers as were given to her when we left our common home.

—Margaret Fuller

I N ESSENCE, WE ARE ALL SPARKS OF THE DIVINE. REALIZING THIS we can accept that the Goddess within each of us is not an untouchable, illusionary figment of our imagination. She is real, an integral part of us, the self that possesses what has been called "female intuition." Resisting and denying the wisdom of our intuition cuts us off from our most precious and feminine features. Thankfully, we are now reclaiming the Goddess within by accepting those aspects of ourselves that respect our intuition.

Until recently the Goddess within many of us had been silenced because we feared her power and had no idea how to wield it lovingly. Fortunately, we are now learning guidelines for expressing her power in constructive ways. Allowing ourselves to know and honor our powerful inner wisdom takes courage, for when we do, not only do we experience the joy of spiritual development, we also have the responsibilities that empowerment and wisdom bring.

We are all entrusted with the light of the Goddess. It is our birthright and responsibility to allow that light to illumine our life's path.

Training the Priestess in Us

MY DEAR FRIEND AND SPIRITUAL MOTHER REFERS TO THE CHALLENGES we face in the school of life as the training of the priestess. Somehow seeing our everyday difficulties in the light of priestess training lends meaning to their teachings.

We all have an understanding, compassionate, and gentle inner priestess who sits beside an artesian well of wisdom. We are in training to recognize and claim that part of ourselves. Being able to call her forth when we need her is to be in touch with our limitless source of wisdom.

Close your eyes and begin to hear the gentle bubbling of spring water. Allow yourself to feel soothed and comforted by the sound. Notice you are by a lovely fountain flowing with crystal clear water. Invite into this sacred place your inner priestess. If you do not feel totally loved by the woman who appears, she is not your priestess. Allow that image to fade and invite your real priestess to be with you. When she appears, spend some time getting to know her and exploring your beautiful surroundings together. She has a gift for you, a vase you can fill with water from the fountain. Ask her if she is willing to guide you on your path. Agree to meet with each other regularly, becoming partners and friends as you train together through difficulties, decisions, and triumphs.

*I welcome the wisdom and compassion
of my inner priestess.*

*I easily accept the valuable lessons
learned in the school of life.*

I am feminine, in the finest sense of the word.

Accepting Our Credibility

HOW OFTEN DO WE HAVE A SMIRKING CYNIC ON OUR SHOULDER saying various versions of "What do you know?" and "Why would people want to hear what you have to say?" Even in the face of compliments, honors, and successes we women seem to question our credibility. Our doubt is fueled by degrading self-talk and the flames of low self-esteem are fanned by repetition.

But we are in charge of our thoughts. Through awareness, affirmations, and healing—changing our self-talk and self-concept—we can diminish the judging voice from a shout to a whisper, eventually replacing it with a loving and supportive inner voice that believes in our credibility. With courage and commitment we can learn to give ourselves the credit we deserve, cut our self-criticism, and accept the idea that what we know and think has value.

You are incredibly competent. If life were a university, what degrees would you have earned thus far and what ones are you now working toward? A B.A. in communication, a B.S. in diplomacy in the workplace, an M.A. in child development, a Ph.D. in the wisdom of experience . . . Take a moment now to write down your degrees.

Then, close your eyes and focus on your breathing for a minute or two. If your mind wanders, gently bring it back to concentrating on your breath. Imagine yourself at the prestigious University of Life impressively gowned and hooded. See a smiling, wise, and loving mentor awarding you the degrees and honors you richly deserve. Receive them graciously, knowing you have earned them and are worthy of each.

*I give myself credit for what I know
and what I am learning.*

I value the wisdom I've gained through experience.

Dethroning the Virgin

WHEN GROWING UP, MANY WOMEN WERE LED TO BELIEVE THE ONLY part of them that was acceptable to nice boys was the virgin. Pure, devoted, perfect, an object of respect and worship—a girl he'd be proud to take home to Mother. Of course bad boys seemed to want something else. How confusing for us if we were heart-thumpingly attracted to the bad boys we were afraid for our mothers to meet. If we were attracted to, or repulsed by, bad boys it was probably because they represented shadowy parts of ourselves that, on our pure pinnacle of pseudo-perfectionism, we were busily disowning—the rebel, harlot, and playful parts in us we felt were unacceptable.

Even as adults we often still carry the belief that, in order to be acceptable, we have to epitomize the ideal of virgin perfection. But we need to begin to understand we aren't, can't, and probably don't even want to be only the virgin. Rather, we can take the good parts of the virgin ideal—such as gentleness and purity of thought—and leave perfectionism behind.

For all of us, dethroning the virgin does not mean banishing her from the palace altogether. It means realizing the virgin in ourselves is a realistic and healthy part of our being—not the whole shebang. As long as the virgin is our only acceptable way of being, or even a large percentage, we set ourselves up to feel ashamed of our imperfections, our very humanness. And shame, in all of its various disguises, does need to be kicked out of the throne room. We do not need to be perfect to be acceptable to ourselves or others.

I have the courage to revel in my humanness.

*I accept all of my different selves
into the throne room of my heart.*

I am perfectly acceptable just the way I am.

Tapping Invisible Power

ALTHOUGH WE MAY THINK OF IT BY DIFFERENT NAMES—GOD, SPIRIT, or Guardian Angel, for example—there is an invisible source of power around and within us waiting for us to call on it when we need it. Too often we ignore this presence out of ignorance, doubt, or forgetfulness.

Annabelle is a person who remembers and uses her power. One dark night the power came to her aid in a dramatic fashion. She was settling down for her first night at a retreat center in the California foothills when she realized she needed something from her car. Carefully making her way, she stepped back into what appeared to be tall grass at the edge of the parking lot. Seconds later she woke up in a six-foot culvert. Wedged in head first, she could not right herself or climb out. Feeling blood on the back of her head, she thought, "No one knows I'm here, and it's midnight." Instead of panicking, she said, "Father, I need your help." Suddenly, with no memory of how it happened, she found herself standing beside her car!

To help you connect with the presence within and around you, close your eyes and allow yourself to move deeply into the center of your being, a place within you that is filled with gratitude for the mysteries of life. As you inhale say, "For your power," and as you exhale say, "I thank you." Gently continue this breath prayer for a few minutes, allowing a sense of peace to fill your heart.

We all possess incredible power. We are invited to have the courage to own it, use it wisely, and be thankful for it.

I tap into the invisible power in and around me.

I am surrounded by forces that love and protect me.

I thankfully accept the love and wisdom of my Goddess within.

Making a Difference

MOTHER TERESA HAS A SAYING THAT EXEMPLIFIES GODDESS ENERGY: "Do small things with great love." My husband expanded this to say, "Doing small things with great love makes a big difference!" All of our lives are filled with literally millions of opportunities to do small things and make a big difference.

One day in Hawaii a ferocious storm washed hundreds of starfish ashore. A woman, on her morning walk, bent down every few steps to throw a starfish back into the sea. A man saw her and commented, "There are so many of the poor things it can't make any real difference for you to throw these few back." With a knowing smile, she tossed another starfish into the water and turning to the man said, "It made a difference to that one."

We can all make a difference. Often we don't even know when we have touched someone's life in a positive manner—a Goddess way. By ministering out of our ordinary experiences—expressing truthfully who we are—we create extraordinary differences in other lives. We all possess the Goddess energy, and when we illuminate a fragment of our own being through understanding and awareness, we naturally light the road for others.

I make a difference.

I do small things with great love.

I express my Goddess energy
by being truly who I am.

Assimilating Both Saber and Scepter

REMEMBER THE CHILD'S RHYME, "WHAT ARE LITTLE GIRLS MADE OF? Sugar and spice and everything nice. What are little boys made of? Frogs and snails and puppy dog tails." As a little girl I used to think, "What a drag. I'd much rather be a boy."

This seemingly harmless little ditty exemplifies what so many of us were taught—that we must be nice and sweet. Hidden in the message was the belief that power and authority were not sweet and nice and thereby were only masculine prerogatives. Both the saber of power and the scepter of authority, or at least an outward show of them, were deemed somehow contradictory to our femininity.

This of course is not so. It takes a lot of strength and power to have a baby, speak our feelings, be intimate, make a living, be a peacemaker, and juggle the many details of everyday life. We women are now beginning to reclaim, outwardly, what we have suspected all along but were afraid to acknowledge—we are strong; we do have power and authority.

Our job now is to have the courage to assimilate the saber of power and the scepter of authority into our lives in a gentle, loving, and feminine way—from an essence of love and a desire for the empowerment of all people, not just a select, safe few. The first step in this process is to love and accept ourselves—our strengths and weaknesses, our power and vulnerabilities. We are each called to take up the saber and the scepter in our own lives.

I am powerful and strong.
I love being a woman.
I use my power and authority
gently and with love.

Serving as a Vessel

A PRIESTESS IS ONE WHO ACTS AS A CHANNEL FOR THE DIVINE—a clear, strong vessel able to hold and disperse spiritual energy. She helps others by sharing what she has learned from the painful struggles in her own life. Using that definition, aren't we all in training to be a priestess?

In order to be a strong and useful vessel we must first endure the potter's fire. Annie, a beautiful and educated woman, works with a hospice bereavement program. People feel safe expressing even their darkest feelings in her presence. She doesn't have to say much; an aura of understanding and acceptance flows from her toward those who are grieving. Why? Because she has been through her personal fire—the death of one of her children—and emerged a stronger and more empathetic vessel for divine energy.

Pain can be an incubator for compassion, as it was for Annie, if we keep our intention toward healing, learning, and serving. When we view our pain as an instrument of growth and an opportunity to, eventually, be better able to serve others, it takes on a greater meaning. As we know, it is easier to endure that which has meaning for us than that which seems totally senseless. Being courageous enough to see painful circumstances in our lives as occasions to perfect the vessel we are allows us to take the meaning of our lives to its highest point.

I reach out to others in empathy and understanding.

I have the courage to find meaning in even my deepest pain.

I see myself as a vessel for divine energy
and find joy in serving others.

Transforming and
Transmuting Circumstances

WHEN MY YOUNGEST SON WAS NINE YEARS OLD, HE AND I WERE riding our bikes along the shoulder of Kalanianiole Highway in Honolulu. Contentedly following my son, I suddenly "saw" in my mind's eye a pickup truck swerve and hit him. I then "saw" myself in the middle of the street holding him while begging someone to call an ambulance. Remembering a formula I'd been taught for transforming and altering circumstances, I prayed, "Father/Mother God, I ask for the transformation and transmutation of what I just saw and for the perfect, right happening to occur instead." At that moment, a red pickup truck swerved onto the shoulder, missing my son by only a few inches.

Often, when we pay close attention, our intuition will give us previews of coming attractions or detractions. Alerted to what may happen, we then have the opportunity to ask for a change in unwanted circumstances. Learning to trust our intuition is one of our most challenging lessons. But when we have the courage to listen to our inner voice and the strength to act on what we hear, we are connecting with the wisdom of the Goddess within.

I pay attention to my intuition.

I have the courage to trust my intuition.

*I use my inner wisdom and power
to alter circumstances.*

Gleaning Wisdom from Silence

WISDOM BEGINS IN SILENCE. AMID THE CLATTER, CLACK, AND cacophony of our usual daily existence, how can we expect to hear the whisper of our wisdom and intuition? Having the courage to discipline ourselves to make time for silence, a time in which we can pay attention, is a real challenge. But unless we do, we will be aware of only a fraction of our selves.

Abraham Kawai, a Hawaiian teacher/healer, says that although his students learn many things, his entire teaching could be summed up in two words—pay attention. Interestingly, the opposite of "attention" is to "disregard and neglect." How often do we disregard our still, small voice—the voice of the Goddess within? How often do we neglect being silent and, therefore, make it impossible to hear the quiet messages she whispers to us concerning what is best for us to do, say, or be?

Take a moment now to listen, to pay attention to your inner voice. Find a place where you will not be disturbed and sit upright in a comfortable position. If you have a question or a problem that needs answering, jot it down on a piece of paper and then keep the paper beside you as you move into this quiet time. Tune in to your breathing, concentrate only on your breath entering and exiting your body. If thoughts intrude, bless them and allow them to effortlessly float out of your mind. Return your attention to your breath.

Do this simple exercise for only as long as it is comfortable. The last minute or two say "I" as you inhale and "know" as you exhale. Very gently open your eyes and randomly write down any thoughts that present themselves to you. They may or may not appear to have any connection to your original question. It doesn't matter. As you become accustomed to letting ideas pour forth freely, you will glean wisdom from the silence.

I pay attention to the Goddess within.
I have all of my answers inside of myself.

Transcending the Trojan Horse

IN THE LEGENDARY TROJAN WAR THE PATRIARCHAL GREEKS overcame the matriarchal Trojans by trickery. The huge Trojan horse, a supposed peace offering from the Greeks, which they said would make Troy impregnable, was invited inside the walls of Troy. As the Trojans slept, Greek troops hidden inside the horse opened the gates to their waiting army. Troy was burned, and the Greeks won the war.

As this parable illustrates, feminine energy has been "asleep" for centuries while masculine energy and values took over religion and politics and became revered as the only way. But we, as modern Trojan women, have awakened to the need for balance in all aspects of our lives and culture. Warlike masculine qualities of dominance, competition, and conquest, untempered by the spiritual and nurturing qualities of the feminine, have finally endangered the very Mother who sustains us—Planet Earth. We must honor, balance, and synthesize both masculine and feminine energy now, in the microcosm of ourselves and the macrocosm of our world.

Take a few moments to list the feminine and masculine qualities you would like to embody. Close your eyes and visualize someone or something that epitomizes the positive masculine qualities. He can be a real person whom you respect and admire or a symbol your wise subconscious presents to you. Invite him to be an honored and valued part of your inner entourage. Do the same visualization for the feminine qualities you wish to personify.

As we move through our days we need to be willing to incorporate both masculine and feminine energy and attributes within ourselves.

I value both my feminine and masculine qualities.

I create peace and harmony on our planet by first creating peace and harmony within myself.

Adopting a Mentor-Mom

WHEN FAMILIES STAYED IN THE SAME TOWN WITH FARMS AND businesses passing from generation to generation, women naturally received love, wisdom, and caring from older women; maybe a mother, grandmother, or wise aunt became a source of inspiration and comfort for a young woman. So often now, however, we are far from family, cut off from relatives by distance or estrangement. Yet the need to glean wisdom from an older woman's experience is very much with us. An older woman can turn from her place on the path ahead of us and shed light on where we are at the moment. She has been there.

If we have the mistaken idea that, in order to be adult and mature, we need to go it alone, we should remember that even the most successful and talented athletes have coaches who guide, encourage, and instruct them. We need coaches, too. It is important that we learn from the example of others who have successfully been down the road we are traveling.

If we don't already have a mentor-mom, we need to begin looking for an older woman whom we admire and trust, a woman into whose lap we can crawl when the going gets tough, and at whose feet (symbolically speaking) we can receive wise guidance. As we grow in age, experience, and wisdom, we can continue the circle of mentoring and sisterhood by extending our hand to a younger woman.

Women have much to give each other. We strengthen our Goddess within when we adopt one or more mentor-moms and bless ourselves in the rays of their love.

I give myself the gift of adopting a mentor-mom.

I welcome_____into my life
as a source of comfort, inspiration, and wisdom.

Doing No Harm

IMAGINE WHAT THE WORLD WOULD BE LIKE IF NO ONE HARMED anything or anyone. Wars would cease, rain forests would flourish, babies would be free of bruises and broken bones, women would not be battling the effects of inequality, criticism, and rejection. How can such a dream become a reality? Beginning with ourselves, we can courageously and consciously adopt the gentle attitude of doing no harm. Before we speak or act, we can stop and ask ourselves, "Will what I am about to say or do harm this person or thing?"

We already, at some conscious or unconscious level, live out the desire to do no harm. We may gently pick up a spider and put it outdoors instead of killing it. Or we may thoughtfully alter a statement we're about to make if we know it may be hurtful. But we need to be sure to include ourselves in this accepting attitude of treating all people and things with respect.

An interesting thing happens as we begin to practice harmless living; an awareness of the sacredness of all existence, ourselves included, begins to dawn on us. We begin to sense the Goddess/God in everything. We begin to experience a reverence for life, both animate and inanimate, that, in turn, creates serenity in our hearts and minds.

By expanding our desire not to harm, we create a powerful pebble-in-the-pond phenomenon. The ever-widening circles of respect and love we create touch countless people.

I am respectful of everything and everyone.
I consciously practice harmless living.
I have reverence for all life.